ANTON VON WEBERN: *PERSPECTIVES*

Terra-cotta bust of Webern by Josef Humplik [*Webern Archive*]

ANTON
VON WEBERN
PERSPECTIVES

Compiled by HANS MOLDENHAUER
Edited by DEMAR IRVINE
Introductory Interview with IGOR STRAVINSKY

Seattle and London, 1966
UNIVERSITY OF WASHINGTON PRESS

Library of Congress Catalog Card Number 66-13539
Printed in the United States of America

Preface

In the history of music in the first half of the twentieth century, a very important place must be conceded to the great Viennese triumvirate: Schoenberg, Webern, Berg. Arnold Schoenberg (1874-1951) was the oldest and the leader of the group. The last eighteen years of his life were spent in the United States, where he exerted a strong influence upon a younger generation of American composers. Among his first pupils and disciples in Vienna were Anton von Webern (born in Vienna, December 3, 1883; died in Mittersill, Austria, September 15, 1945), and Alban Berg (1885-1935). These two lived out their lives on Austrian soil.

During his lifetime, Webern was the most neglected of the three. For some, perhaps, death and immortality must go hand in hand. This need not be said of Schoenberg, who was a strong and vigorous champion of his own music. But Berg was not fully appreciated until after his early death. And for Webern, it was really only after the conclusion of World War II and his own tragic end that he came into his own. All at once his music seemed important—prophetic. Significant of this growing interest was the recording by Robert Craft, in the mid-fifties, of all the known works of Webern, and their issue through Columbia Records in 1958.

In 1962, the First International Webern Festival was held in Seattle on May 25-28, under the auspices of the School of Music of the University of Washington. That occasion saw the founding of the International Webern Society. The Second International Webern Festival took place at Salzburg and Mittersill in 1965. Three concerts in commemoration of Anton von Webern were given August 2-3 as an official part of the Salzburg Festival 1965, and a concert and ceremonies at Mittersill on August 4-5 were sponsored by the International Webern Society.

The present volume has grown out of the First International Webern Festival of 1962, and will contribute, it is hoped, to an understanding of Webern and his music. The events of the Festival itself, which proved to be a rewarding experience, deserve to be placed briefly here on record.

Hans Moldenhauer has explained, in "A Webern Archive in America," how he came to acquire a portion of Webern's musical estate. At that time Dr. Moldenhauer was a member of the faculty of the University of Washington School of Music. By the end of September, 1961, he had impressed upon his colleagues of the School of Music the desirability of sponsoring a Webern festival, in which the previously unknown works should be heard, along with a generous sampling of the works with opus numbers, and some representative compositions showing Webern's influence on the following generation.

To plan a festival within the space of eight months was a tremendous undertaking, but Dr. Moldenhauer, as chairman of the Festival Committee—which also included Dr. Stanley Chapple, then Director of the School of Music, and Professors John T. Moore, Warren Babb, James Beale, Else Geissmar, and Demar Irvine—displayed such extraordinary organizational talent that the miracle was accomplished. The University of Washington administration, always friendly toward the arts, gave warm support and generous assistance, especially President Charles E. Odegaard, Provost Frederick P. Thieme, Dean Solomon Katz, and Dean Joseph L. McCarthy. Many who assisted in various ways in the planning and execution of the Festival must remain anonymous, but mention should be made of the strong moral support received from the Northwest Chapter (of which James Beale was then president) of the International Society for Contemporary Music, and the Northwestern Chapter (Miriam Terry, then chairman) of the American Musicological Society.

Of the many persons called upon to participate, some were at the University of Washington and some were at far distant places. From week to week one could sense, through both the local activity and the flood of correspondence from afar, the mounting enthusiasm for this tribute to Anton von Webern. The devoted interest in Webern's music, once shared by only a few, had spread among a younger generation, and the Festival provided a focus for the expression of their enthusiasm. The inspired dedication of the performers was communicated to those who came as spectators, and the whole atmosphere—the *Stimmung*—was that of an experience in which one was caught up and absorbed. The Festival was indeed a magnificent tribute to a great composer. Webern's message was clear and eloquent, and touched us profoundly.

By a fortunate coincidence, the Philadelphia Orchestra, directed by Eugene Ormandy, gave a pair of concerts in Seattle's superb new opera house on May 24 and 25, 1962. The booking was arranged by the Seattle Symphony Orchestra as a part of its contribution to the Seattle World's Fair ("Century 21") then in progress. Mr. Ormandy, who from the start had expressed a lively interest in the newly uncovered Webern compositions, conducted the world premiere of *Im Sommerwind* at the May 25 concert.

During the following three days and evenings, the campus of the University of Washington was the setting for a series of concerts, public lectures, a scholars' symposium, official luncheons, a Webern Memorial Exhibition of manuscripts and documents from the Moldenhauer Archive, and the organizational meeting of the International Webern Society. Guest of honor throughout was Mrs. Amalie Webern Waller, Webern's daughter, who had flown from Vienna for the occasion.

At the concerts, all of Webern's works then in the Moldenhauer Archive and predating Opus I were presented *en bloc,* with the exception of *Siegfrieds Schwert.* Approximately one-half of Webern's previously known *oeuvre* was also given, namely, Opera 2, 3, 4, 5, 7, 8, 11, 12, 14, 15, 16, 17, 23, 25, 27, and 29. The performing artists who participated exhibited a singleness of purpose and wholehearted dedication which no mere words of recognition could adequately express. It was through their willingness and cooperation that a sampling of works by other contemporary composers could be included among the Festival concerts.

Esther LaBerge and Dr. Rudolph Ganz, of Chicago, undertook the world premières of fourteen of Webern's early songs, in three groups: *Three Poems* (1899-1903), *Eight Early Songs* (1901-4), and *Three Avenarius Songs* (1903-4). In addition, for one of the matinée concerts Esther LaBerge sang two of the monologues from Frank Martin's *Jedermann,* and Dr. Ganz played a group of Debussy piano preludes.

Grace-Lynne Martin, from California, besides the world première of *Five Dehmel Songs* (1906-8), prepared Opera 3, 14, 15, and 16. Her collaborator in the works requiring piano was Leonard Stein, while for Opera 14, 15, 16, Dr. Stanley Chapple rehearsed and directed the ensemble.

Ethel Casey, soprano from Raleigh, North Carolina, sang Opus 17 (with ensemble directed by Stanley Chapple), Opera 23 and 25 (with pianist Walter Golde), and the solo part in the *Cantata,* Opus 29. For one of the matinée concerts Miss Casey, accompanied by Walter Golde, sang the "Lied der Lulu" from Alban Berg's *Lulu,* the aria that Berg had dedicated to Webern.

Leonard Stein, eloquent pianistic champion of contemporary music as well as editor of Schoenberg's writings and compositions, generously gave his experienced advice in the preparation of various Webern works for performance. He closed the first evening concert with the *Variations for Piano,* Opus 27, and on

May 28 presented a notable recital of post-Webern music, including the following pieces: *Cantéyodjayâ* (1948), by Olivier Messiaen; *Piano Pieces I, V, VIII* (1953-55), by Karlheinz Stockhausen; *Third Sonata* (1957), by Pierre Boulez; *Calligraphy* (1960), by Keijiro Satō; *Partitions for Piano* (1957), by Milton Babbitt; *Composition for Piano* (1960), by Robert Taylor; *Six Bagatelles for Piano,* Opus 29 (1960), by James Beale; and *Sechs Vermessene* (1958), by Ernst Krenek.

The University of Washington String Quartet, consisting of Professors Emanuel Zetlin, Richard Ferrin, Vilem Sokol, and Eva Heinitz, presented the world premières of Webern's *String Quartet* (1905) and *Langsamer Satz* (1905). This group also contributed Opus 5 and Opus 9 to the program and, together with Dr. Stanley Chapple as pianist, the *Quintet* (1906).

The University of Washington Collegium Musicum, under the guidance of Professors Miriam Terry and Gerald Kechley, prepared Opus 2 and Opus 29. They were joined in the *Cantata* by Ethel Casey, soprano, and a specially selected orchestra.

Other Webern works heard at the first matinée concert were: Opus 4 and Opus 12 (Emilie Berendsen Bloch, mezzo-soprano; David Bloch, piano); Opus 7 (Hazelle Thomas Miloradovitch, violin; Donald Anthony, piano); Opus 11 (Eugene Wilson, cello; David Bloch, piano).

For music in the post-Webern idiom, the Society for the Performance of Contemporary Music of San Francisco, founded in 1960, sent a contingent of young composers and performers. Among the works heard at the two matinée concerts were *Sonata for Bassoon and Piano,* by Leland Smith, played by the composer and William Bolcom, pianist; *Seriatim* for solo violin, by Christopher Lantz, played by Mrs. Miloradovitch; William Bolcom's *Fantasy-Sonata for Piano,* played by the composer, who also performed *Impromptu et Variations II,* by the French composer Henri Pousseur. These concerts also included performances of Schoenberg's Opus 19, played by John Ringgold, piano; and of

Ernst Krenek's *Fourth Piano Sonata,* played by David Burge.

The Festival provided an appropriate occasion for the organizational meeting (May 27) of the International Webern Society, in which considerable interest had already been expressed. In a subsequent ballot by mail, the following were elected as the society's first officers and directors: President, Hans Moldenhauer (U.S.A.); First Vice President, Paul Collaer (Belgium); Second Vice President, Leonard Stein (U.S.A.); Secretary, Paul A. Pisk (U.S.A.); Treasurer, Warren Babb (U.S.A.); Directors, Pierre Boulez (France), Luigi Dallapiccola (Italy), Rudolf Kolisch (U.S.A.), Ernst Krenek (U.S.A.), Willi Reich (Switzerland), Eduard Steuermann (U.S.A.), Igor Stravinsky (U.S.A.).

The complete documentation of the First International Webern Festival went into the Moldenhauer Archive, where it can be retrieved as needed. Notable among the contents of this material are the literally hundreds of messages of good will, often containing statements of some significance, from those who were unable to attend; a fine lecture by Alfred V. Frankenstein, music and art critic of the *San Francisco Chronicle,* on "Music Criticism: What It Is and What It Isn't"; clippings of press reviews; the excellent program notes by Edwin H. Schloss for *Im Sommerwind;* reminiscences by Ruzena Herlinger and Rudolph Ganz; and statements of impressions that remained several months after the Festival from a number of participants, including Amalie Webern Waller, Leonard Stein, Grace-Lynne Martin, and Ethel Casey.

The present volume may be said to contain the more permanent results of the First International Webern Festival in terms of critical, biographical, and documentary material of interest to the growing numbers of scholars, musicians, and listeners concerned with Webern's music.

Igor Stravinsky, unable to attend the Festival because of other commitments, nevertheless expressed an interest in the project from its inception. We are deeply indebted to him for his willingness to provide an introduction to the volume in the form of an interview, "A Decade Later." Mr. Stravinsky's independence of schools and trends is one of the notable musical phenomena of our century. He views the scene with a kind of Olympian detachment, strongly laced with candor and justice, and with vision unclouded by partisanship. Those works of the 1950's—notably the *Canticum Sacrum, Agon,* and *Threni*—were, after all, pure Stravinsky. At the same time, they demonstrate irrevocably that the composer understood Webern profoundly.

In Seattle, the keynote of the Festival was set by Ernst Krenek in his address, "Anton Webern: A Profile." Although he now resides in California, Dr. Krenek was born in Vienna and was a pupil of Franz Schreker. He experimented with several styles and achieved great success while still in his twenties. One of the ablest proponents of twelve-tone music, Dr. Krenek has been closely involved with the progress of contemporary music as composer, conductor, author, and lecturer. "New Dimensions of Music" is a condensed version of his second public address at the Festival.

"Webern's Musical Estate," by James Beale, of the University of Washington School of Music, gives a general account of the pre-Opus 1 works. Professor Beale assumed major editorial responsibility for insuring that many of these works were properly transcribed from the autographs for use at the Festival.

Paul Amadeus Pisk, composer and musicologist, was in former years a pupil of Schoenberg and very much a part of the Viennese scene. His discussion of "Webern's Orchestral Works" concentrates largely upon *Im Sommerwind,* with a helpful analysis of its main features. Dr. Pisk was for many years active at the University of Texas, and more recently has been at Washington University in St. Louis.

"Webern's *Dehmel Lieder* of 1906-8" are considered by Leonard Stein as representing the threshold of a new expression in the composer's career. Together with Grace-Lynne Martin, Mr. Stein recreated these songs at the Festival.

Wallace McKenzie (Wayland Baptist College, Plainview, Texas) brought to the Festival the fresh viewpoints of a specialist who had recently completed a substantial doctoral dissertation on the music of Webern. In his essay on "Webern's Technique of Choral Composition" he demonstrates, I think, that there are many facets to Webern's music, and that we will go on discussing Webern for years to come, just as we discuss other great composers, without running out of interesting subject matter.

William Austin, professor of music at Cornell University, refers us to the mainstream of music history in his consideration of "Webern and the Tradition of the Symphony." Professor Austin has included a penetrating chapter on Webern in his new book on twentieth-century music (Norton).

Leland Smith (Stanford University), who is both a composer and a perceptive theorist, engages in a more technical discussion of certain works in "Composition and Precomposition in the Music of Webern." In seeking to explain how this music is constructed, his aim is to see not merely the trees but the whole delightful grove. For those readers who may still find a Webern score somewhat confusing, Professor Smith's analysis should prove most helpful.

It is a pleasure here to reproduce the interesting communications of Egon Wellesz and Cesar Bresgen which were read at official luncheons of the Festival. What is so touching about these messages is the clear glimpse we receive of Webern, the man, as seen through the eyes of two of his friends. Dr. Wellesz, a contemporary of Webern in the Viennese days, was one of the very first group of Schoenberg's disciples. He later shifted the scene of his activity to Oxford University, and he is one of the most learned and eminent musicologists of our time. Professor Bresgen is now very active at the Academie Mozarteum in Salzburg.

"A Webern Archive in America" reveals in explicit detail the nature and extent of that portion of the Moldenhauer Archive relating specifically to Anton von Webern. The entire Moldenhauer Archive is an impressive and far-ranging collection which is still actively growing. Inquiries regarding the holdings should be addressed to Dr. Hans Moldenhauer, 808 South Lincoln Street, Spokane, Washington 99204.

The editor assumes responsibility for the imperfections in the Selected Bibliography and the Reference List of Webern's Works, and expresses his thanks to the contributors for their cooperation in reviewing, and in some cases revising, their manuscripts, and for their patience during the long period of preparation for the press.

The illustrations, selected from materials in the Moldenhauer Archive, are here published, to the best of our knowledge, for the first time.

DEMAR IRVINE

December, 1965
Seattle, Washington

Contents

Illustrations

IGOR STRAVINSKY: An Interview

Introduction: A Decade Later

> When sounds are smooth and clear, and have a single pure tone, then they are not relatively but absolutely beautiful.
> Plato, *Philebus,* 51

> Music unites the contrary attributes of being both intelligible and untranslatable.
> Lévi-Strauss, *Le cru et le cuit*

University of Washington Interviewer: You were complaining about Anton-olatry, Mr. Stravinsky, and asserting that it is time to replace cultism with criticism.

I.S.: Yes, but we should not altogether despise cults. As prime movers they are far more useful than critics, after all, and in Webern's case the cult, rather than the critics, is responsible for much of our knowledge of the music. But cults tend to become dome-shaped, and domes exclude the light. Worse still, the Webern cult made the mistake of switching from the music to the musician, a barren devotion in any case, but especially so in this one because of the unexploitable nature of the mahatma-to-be. The pendulum has started back, though, and there are signs of tastes and discriminations coming into operation. Soon we will have to listen from a new angle. But poor Webern!

U.W.I.: What do you mean by that?

I.S.: I was merely musing on the destiny of composers and the depredations of amateur appraisers with their cycles of inflation and deflation. The fact that Webern is suffering from the latter at present is simply the result of an oversupply of simulacrums produced by cheap, or rather—since Foundation wages are generous—superficial labor. No doubt even the thought of such a commerce would have horrified the composer, but the heliocentric position accorded him (above Schoenberg!) by, for example, the *Domaine musical* with its anti-Brahms deaf spot (and, hence, the Brahmsian heredity in Schoenberg) would have given him a mortal shock. Nothing was more absurd in those appraisers of a decade ago than the Schoenberg-Webern syzygy. Over to you, U.W.I.

U.W.I.: Do you think the state of the market is the only reason for the deflation, Mr. Stravinsky, or were we guilty of some inflating of Webern himself?

I.S.: Whether or not our estimations of Webern were somewhere askew is not of great moment. There is nothing surprising in errors of musical judgment in confrontation with the radically new. What does amaze is the wholesale commission of that most obvious of mistakes, the attempt to multiply originality. The more original and individual, so the more unrepeatable and inimitable, yet multiplication quickly became the *carte de jour,* not only of "abstract structural devices," as music reviewers are fond of scribbling (and what musical device is not abstract and structural?) but even of the tone of voice. I know something about pseudo-Webern for at the time it was being manufactured I came under the spell of him myself, though I think I was faithful to Webern, to my discoveries in him, longer than anyone else.

U.W.I.: Are you suggesting that others who found their direction in him have betrayed him?

I.S.: Not that, not that. I would say, however, that the group which sprang from him and into prominence in the fifties now tends to regard him too lightly, as something they like to call a "precursor," a tugboat which, now that it has brought to shore such mighty liners as themselves, may be sent to rest in shallow waters (where for company it will find a few old skiffs like myself). At times I have had the impression that they still program his "precursory" music along with the grander confections of their own establishments simply to show how they have "turned it to account," or given it more "scope." At any rate there is no doubt that their improvements are meant to supersede, the authors of them having already acknowledged the futility of those cranky old "serial" formulas Webern was so obsessed with, and consigned them to completed history (Vienna between the wars, according to the dates on the tombstone). Disregarding the fact that in the absence of other differentia it is an unarguable proposition whether "serial" music represents a decline from the previous stage, today's progressives have formed a coalition with yesterday's nonstarters, and we may expect to be hearing again from the latter about the substitution of an "arbitrary order" (those Draconian twelve-tone laws) for a "natural gravitational system," as if both the arbitrary and the natural were not equally artificial and composed. Like all *ars nova/ars antiqua* debates, however, this one is of little use to practicing composers, and as always the music to come will be determined by other factors than the rules of the rule makers.

U.W.I.: To go back to the question of scope, Mr. Stravinsky, do you consider Webern's to be too narrow?

I.S.: Not for Webern—which is no answer, of course, but I cannot understand the word in musical terms. Webern's time scale is tiny, his quantity is minute, the variety of his forms is small, but whether these are measurements of scope I am unable to say. If, for example, scope is also a question of depth and not merely of width and expanse, then Webern's can be very great, and it is in any case perfectly circumscribed, which I say to remind you that we can only judge what the composer has done, not what he did not set out to do. But can we be certain, to begin with, that the scope we are looking for is really Webern's and not your own Beethovenesque idea of what it should be? Admittedly, Webern often seems to have put a low premium on his listener's sense of involvement. His music is wholly unrhetorical and in that sense unpersuasive. There is no movement from simple to complex, no development of subsidiary parts or integration of counterthemes, second subjects, fugal episodes, and the like. The listener is definitely not invited to participate in the argument of the creation as he is in the symphonies of Beethoven. On the contrary, each opus offers itself only as a whole, a unity to be contemplated. Now obviously such an artwork is essentially static, and obviously, too, the cost in subjectivity is high. Naturally I concede that it is possible to feel constricted when listening to a succession of, especially, the very short pieces, and to attribute this feeling to lack of scope, but I consider the very attempt to follow a chain of, as I say, unities, to be a quantitative mistake; I mean, just because they are clock-time short. For a test you must try the single opus and in a neighborhood of other music. Thus, in Venice a few years ago I heard the Parennin Quartet struggle through some forty minutes of Boulez' *Livre pour quatuor,* then play the four minutes of Webern's *Bagatelles.* I assure you that since then scope has never seemed to be a matter of size.

U.W.I.: What are your present criticisms of the music, Mr. Stravinsky?

I.S.: They are mere differences of palate, mostly, and doubtless more revealing of myself than of Webern. Those *molto ritenuto, molto espressivo,* and "dying away" phrase endings weary me now, and there is a touch of cuteness in the vocal music that I dislike: the too frisky piano figure at the beginning of *"Wie bin ich froh!"* for instance, and the *"Glück"* at the conclusion of the Chinese choruses, though the *chinoiserie* is also less subtle than in the early Li-Tai-Po song, and in fact the whole opus reminds me of a musical snuffbox; but the worst example is surely that wretched *"Bienchen"* in *Gleich und Gleich* (did Webern know Hugo Wolf's setting of this poem?) which should have been a large wasp with a good sting. These are minor dyslogistics, however, simple conflicts of temperament which you will understand better when I add that I also prefer unhappiness to happiness and misery to gay spirits in a great deal of German music besides Webern, since, and emphatically including, *Die Meistersinger*.

U.W.I.: But do you have other, more basic, criticisms, or larger criticisms of specific pieces, that you had not felt a decade ago?

I.S.: The *String Quartet* left me with a slight feeling of aridity when I heard it recently, but if the performance had been better my report of the music might have been very different. Then the saxophone *Quartet*, when I heard it last in Paris a few seasons ago, sounded somewhat soiled by the years in the first movement, and somewhat scatty in the second. This performance was poor also, but only part of the blame can be laid to it, I think, for the hammering succession of downbeats that labor the second movement are also the fault of the notation: the note values are too large and the measures too small. As you know, the silent or suspended beat with the notes on the anacrusis is one of the devices of this movement that Webern was to employ again in later works, though with a degree of success that is still hotly contended. Its formation near the end of the *Concerto* disturbs no one, but many think the use of it in the final twelve measures of the piano *Variations* mere *Papiermusik*, owing to attenuating changes of tempo. The metrical accent obtains here only if the listener is looking at a score or watching a conductor, they argue, and therefore toward the end of the passage the ear perceives the notes not in relation to silent beats but as beats themselves.

Another criticism I might mention is that sometimes Webern's choral harmony strikes me oddly, for example the "*Im Dunkel*" near the end of the *First Cantata*, and the parallel-interval passages in the fifth movement of the *Second Cantata*. I think I see the interval logic and the "purity" of these constructions, and I am at least willing to believe that they derive from a "teleological" conception (in practice, a mania for total identification) of the form. But it *is* harmony, after all, even when described as a "refracted expression of the horizontal interval structure" (a commentator's concettism), and in the case of the "*Im Dunkel*" it is very banal harmony indeed.

U.W.I.: You have acknowledged that the quality of a performance is vital. How, in your opinion, have performance standards changed in the last decade?

I.S.: But there have *been* far too few performances, apart from the *Five Pieces for String Quartet* and the *Six Pieces for Orchestra,* to allow anyone to speak of "standards." It is worth repeating, though, that performance can make the 100-per-cent difference of comprehension, in this music, as it can no longer do in the case of a popular classic, and even with such a simple and accessible piece as my own *Symphonies of Wind Instruments,* I would not have blamed anyone who had taken it for an ugly duckling on the strength of its London debut (though I see that I have launched an unsuitable metaphor, for the work is no swan even when perfectly played). The other day, leafing through programs of the concerts of Jean Wiener and others in Paris in the early twenties I was surprised to discover that songs and chamber music by Webern had been performed together with some of my own music. I have no recollection of it, however, not even of a circumstantial nature such as whether the few squeaks and twitches the music was then generally reputed to be excited any derision;[1] and I can account for this blank only by doubting the performances. As an idea of what they could have been like I refer you to a recording of the *Bagatelles* made a quarter of a century later (Dial Records, 1950) by the Kolisch Quartet. Here the performers were the highest authorities, the ideal interpreters from the very *sanctum sanctorum* of the composer, yet their performance fails even

[1] This nonawareness of Webern is especially painful to me now that I read him in a letter to Berg dated June 9, 1919: "Strawinsky *war herrlich. Wunderbar sind diese Lieder. Mir geht dieser Musik ganz unglaublich nahe. Ich liebe die ganz besonders. Etwas so unsäglich Rührendes wie diese Wiegenlieder. Wie diese drei Klarinetten klingen! Und* 'Pribaoutki.' *Ah, mein lieber, etwas ganz herrlich! Diese Wörtlichkeit (realismus) führt ins Metaphysiche. Strawinsky-Lieder waren ausserordentlich gelungen.*"

on the level of accuracy. Now I beg you not to misunderstand me. I do not intend this as criticism of the players, who were in fact far ahead of any others at that time in their mastery and understanding of the music. It is, rather, a contribution to the history of performance, and the example can be made again with the Boulez recording of the Webern *Symphony*—at a much less remote date—and with Columbia's "complete" Webern, now twelve years since the making. These efforts are mere curiosities now, studies of the performance limitations (and possibilities) of the time rather than revelations of the music, though on occasion they were that, too, even if only, in some cases, as maps to still undiscovered treasure.

U.W.I.: To me the "curious" aspect of the Columbia recordings is that some of the pieces actually received their first auditions this way, among them the Goethe choruses which, judging by the difficulties of the music even now, must have been a baptism of fire. But the prediction, published in that album, that the *Six Pieces for Orchestra* would become a conductors' Bucephalus, while most of the other music languished, has come all too true.

I.S.: The Columbia project, to which I was witness at every stage, is an incredible chapter of music history, one that makes a decade seem a very long time. To begin with, as most of the musical materials, scores, and parts, did not exist, the conductor had to extract them himself from poor photostats of the original manuscripts; the publishers were eventually obliged to print the music because of the demand created by the recordings. A second difficulty was in the fact that while chamber music could be rehearsed in conjunction with concerts (rehearsals for recordings directly must be paid for at full recording rates), the orchestral music could not be rehearsed at all because the conductor had no orchestral concerts. The only recourse was to rehearse each player individually until everyone had learned his own part like a cipher; and this is in fact what the conductor did, for the three cantatas, the orchestra *Variations*, the *Six Pieces*, the *Passacaglia*, the *Ricer-*

car, and the *Symphony* had to be and were recorded in only two three-hour periods. A third handicap was the absence of any assistance from a musical or engineering supervisor. Not only the musical performance, therefore, but every aspect of the production as well was the responsibility of the conductor. Still, recording companies can hardly be expected to believe in such ventures, and they are no more to blame, certainly, than the conductors who had orchestras and who could have found the money to purchase the time, but who lacked imagination. In this context of my little history it now seems unfair to complain that in some of the performances notes were not always played as nodes, yet I wonder when we will again hear such better-than-violin distinctions of pitch as those of Miss Marni Nixon. (Not from Miss Nixon herself, to be sure: she has graduated from Webern to Liza Doolittle!)

U.W.I.: As you have noted some of your criticism, Mr. Stravinsky, would you also evaluate the high points?

I.S.: After the *Five Movements* and the *Six Pieces,* the next peaks come a decade later, with the Trakl songs, the Canons, the *Volkstexte,* the clarinet and guitar songs. But for me, the *Trio,* the *Symphony,* and the orchestra *Variations* are Webern's greatest achievements.

U.W.I.: Has your estimation of Webern's position changed appreciably in the last decade, Mr. Stravinsky?

I.S.: Not mine, but certainly that of many others. "With it" composers have now turned away, or developed away, from his influence, though their music often continues to be a *catalogue raisonné* of derivations from his. But all of us owe something to him, if not in rhythmic vocabulary then in our sensibility to musical time, for I think Webern has raised everyone's sense of refinement in this regard (well, *nearly* everyone's). Whether there are "great," or only new and very individual, feelings in his music is a question I can answer only for myself, but for me Webern *has* a power to move, and no moment in contemporary music has haunted me more than the coda of the *Symphony*. In spite of what I said at the beginning of our talk, then, if you are seeking strange gods you might do worse than continue to revere St. Anton.

Hollywood, November 5, 1965

ANTON VON WEBERN: *PERSPECTIVES*

ERNST KRENEK

Anton von Webern: A Profile

There is no other composer of similar significance in the whole history of music whose entire life's work (as left by himself to posterity) takes not more than about three hours of performing time, as does that of the Austrian Anton von Webern. Of Webern's thirty-one officially numbered works only his last, a cantata, is a little longer than ten minutes. The shortest lasts less than two minutes. But the small size of Webern's compositions is not the only unusual aspect of the composer's personality and work. While alive, he was highly respected by a few colleagues and experts, but his music was very little known at large, and the majority of those who came into contact with it turned away in anger or derision, despising its originator as the most insane among a group of mentally disturbed modern composers, and his work as even worse than the most exasperating excesses of Arnold Schoenberg, among whose original disciples Webern belonged.

And yet, immediately after Webern's untimely death in 1945 his influence upon a younger generation of musicians spread with incredible intensity and speed, until even such a master as Igor Stravinsky in his advanced years adopted many of Webern's ideas and adapted them to his own creative purposes. But not only do young composers from subarctic Lapland to down-under Australia revere Webern as the fountainhead of their stylistic and theoretical essays; his music has also been received with genuine enthusiasm by audiences in all countries. It is not yet as widely played as more conventional contemporary exercises in composition, partly because it confronts the performer with unusual demands; but, whenever it is played, listeners are fascinated and moved.

The brevity of Webern's musical utterance bewildered audiences that were used to the expansive, explicit, exuberant, and repetitious style of the late Romantic period, as seen in the works of Wagner, Strauss, the contemporary Russians, and some of the French impressionists. But what really shocked them was the terrific degree of concentration in Webern's music, which seemed to reduce musical matter to a few drops of precious essence. For the first time in its history, music became so lean and transparent that its single elements seemed to float in isolation between frightening air pockets of total silence. Not only each tone, but also its inflection, its precise dynamic level, its manner of vanishing into nothingness, took on unheard-of, almost frightful significance.

It is not difficult to understand that people reacted to Webern's music with anguish, dismay, and frequently hysterical laughter. They were accustomed to the catchy tunes of Italian opera; the nobly sentimental discourse of Chopin; the thundering, heated eloquence of Wagner; the expansive gestures of Strauss; and above all to solid continuity in any musical process. Especially in Austria, which was attuned to the massive weightiness of Bruckner, the grandiose architecture of Mahler, the dashing sweep of the Strauss waltzes, and the lackadaisical lilt of Léhar's operettas, Webern was looked upon almost as a subversive character. Persons who held such opinions—and there were many of them in high places even in the 1930's—were startled when I told them that I found Webern's music eminently Austrian, as far as it makes any sense to apply such characteristics to music at all. But if a listener is inclined toward associative ideas, he might easily find that Webern's music evokes the clear, thin air and the formidable, tense silence of the very high mountain summits.

Who was the man who wrote this extraordinary music? Anton von Webern was born in 1883, the offspring of a family of the lower nobility—titled country squires who owned some small estate in the Austrian mountains. I still see the bewildered expression on the face of one of the keepers of tradition when he wondered aloud how a man from such a good family could write such horrid music. While this music went far beyond the limits of anything known so far, Webern's life was externally uneventful until his violent death. He studied musicology at the University of Vienna, and his intimate knowledge of the intricate rhythmic order and complicated texture of medieval and Renaissance music, of which he edited an important volume (the *Choralis Constantinus* of Heinrich Isaac), is clearly reflected in many aspects of his own work.

Webern's very early works (opus numbers between zero and one), most of which were performed at the First International Webern Festival, are certainly long-winded and loquacious when compared to the concise and terse style so typical of the mature composer. The models that can be recognized are predictably Wagner, Strauss, Mahler, and, in the *String Quartet*—the most accomplished, interesting, and attractive of these youthful attempts—early Schoenberg, with whom Webern began to study in 1904 and remained closely associated for twenty years. Here we find for the first time indications such as *"mit innigstem und ganz zartem Ausdruck," "so zart wie möglich," "ganz leise"*—instructions so typical of Webern's later style, and in striking contrast to the brassy trifle *Siegfrieds Schwert*, written only two years earlier, which sounds more like a beer-drinking song for a German students' fraternity than a composition by the master who was to be at his most eloquent when he depicted silence and stillness.

Webern earned his living in various positions as a conductor of opera, orchestra, and choir, but this was definitely a sideline. He was much too sensitive and introverted for a career that requires social exuberance and outgoing showmanship. His conducting was also somewhat erratic; for, while he at times could convey extraordinary revelations that became unforgettable experiences, at other times the result sounded as if his mind had been on something else—as it probably was.

As an interpreter of music, Webern was an implacable perfectionist—an attitude characteristic of all of Schoenberg's disciples and associates in the shortlived Verein für musikalische Privataufführungen in Vienna around 1920. The demands Webern made upon himself and his musicians were so severe that frequently the purpose of such efforts, that is, the presentation of the music, was jeopardized and nothing was accomplished. And, just as he could in endless rehearsals brood over a few seemingly simple measures, he would also in his analytical lectures, which he gave off and on in small private circles, dwell for hours on minute details. It is clear that these activities did not substantially contribute to his livelihood.

When the Nazis came to power, even this source of modest income dried up, and Webern spent his life in his little house near Vienna, not exactly in poverty, but in very strained and depressing circumstances. He was a quiet, friendly man, but given to sudden, terrifying tantrums. Such outbursts of frightful anguish were undoubtedly caused by pent-up feelings of frustration and bitterness, natural in a man who knew his worth and could convince hardly anybody of it.

There were other conflicts of various kinds besetting the sensitive soul of the composer. It has frequently been questioned whether Webern was actually a religious person, as one might conclude from the fact that in his vocal works he frequently used religious texts, and nearly always words carrying metaphysical connotations, or whether such choice was of a purely literary nature, reflecting conventional concepts of seriousness and high dignity of subject matter, without committing the writer to its contents. Although it would have been difficult to draw the reserved, introverted man into a discussion of such affairs, we never doubted the genuine, profound religiosity of the composer, notwithstanding the fact that formally it was perhaps not always strictly defined. We also had at times the feeling that he suffered because of the officially antireligious stand of the Social-Democratic Party upon which he depended for his livelihood for many years; for this political party was the only agency that would recognize Webern as an artist, entrusting him with the direction of the workers' symphony orchestra and choral organization. Loyalty and gratitude toward his enthusiastic sponsors were at variance with his doubts in regard to some of their philosophical tenets.

Such conflicts are reflected in the extraordinary tension that characterizes his music, especially of his middle period. The tangible results of Webern's creative work between 1917 and 1927 are six groups of altogether twenty-four songs, which last in their entirety twenty-two minutes and thirteen seconds. In this period of ten years Webern turned from the freely improvising style of his earlier works to the discipline of the twelve-tone technique, a move which had far-reaching consequences as it ushered in the present practice of composition described as serial music. As is well known, the twelve-tone technique imposes a great deal of discipline upon the act of composing, since the composer chooses a particular arrangement of the twelve tones of our scale in order to use it consistently throughout the course of his composition as a generator of every single detail of the musical process.

It is interesting that Webern's music, as he comes closer to this very strict organizational procedure, becomes increasingly more expressionistic. The texture of the music is rent by crevices like an ancient glacier in the Alps; the voice line moves in formidable skips, as if bent upon expressing pain and suffering of fantastic intensity. This, at face value, is strangely at variance with the seemingly simple character of the texts of these songs, which are basically religious—either taken from the Scriptures in the Latin version used by the Roman Church, or based on ancient German folk poetry which expresses religious sentiments in the rough-hewn idioms of bygone days. Here, as an example, is one of the poems of the *Five Sacred Songs* (Opus 15):

Arise in the name of the Lord,
Walk toward the Lord,
Step before the Lord,
Pray to the heavenly Father,
That He may forearm us
With three seraphim:
The first to lead us,
The second to feed us,
The third to protect us and shield us,
So that naught may befall our bodies and souls.

This beautifully simple archaic prayer receives from Webern's hand a treatment that evokes the tortured lines of either Gothic or Baroque religious art.

Even more startling is the style of the second group, the *Five Canons on Latin Texts* (Opus 16). The text of the first canon is the well-known "*Christus factus est pro nobis obediens usque ad mortem, mortem autem crucis*" ("Christ for us became obedient unto death, even the death of the Cross"). These words, which for the average Christian have a solemn, ceremonial ring, reflect in Webern's musical setting, in the hectic declamation of the voice, the formidable skips in the melodic line, the skeletonlike leanness of texture, and the acidity of the dissonant combinations, the awesome tragedy actually implied in this seemingly matter-of-fact statement. But at the same time, in spite of the ostensible fierceness of the expression, the music is disciplined in the strictest manner imaginable.

The next step on this road leads Webern to the twelve-tone technique, which Arnold Schoenberg had developed in those years. The later groups of songs derive their substance from twelve-tone rows set up by the composer beforehand. In character these songs generally resemble those of the earlier groups. The texture, however, becomes more involved, and the rhythmic combinations very intricate, because the metric beats are subdivided differently in the several strands of the musical fabric. Groups of three tones stand frequently against groups of two and four, and the texture is further complicated through silences, isolated offbeat tones, syncopations, and the like. The sound colors are highly rarefied throughout all these cycles of songs. The conventional instruments, such as violin and clarinet, are used preferably in very high or very low registers. In the violin part much use is made of plucking, playing near the bridge, playing on mute, and other effects designed to replace the customary sound of the instrument by more remote colorations. A small clarinet is employed for very high piercing tones. The percussive metallic ring so typical of much of the most recent music is supplied by harp, guitar, and celesta.

While in Webern's earlier works the musical matter is frequently made to sound like the weird, awesome, and mysterious rumbles of nature itself—the frightful pounding of hidden volcanoes, or of the soaring winds from other planets—in his middle period the emphasis lies upon extremely sensitive, nervous alertness to the minute movements of the soul, which are magnified through the intensity of the music to inspire anxieties of a different kind. More concerned with human tragedy than with nature's mystery, Webern's music becomes more complex in its texture, more rapid, and still more condensed.

The canon—that is, the strict imitation of a statement in one part by other parts at different pitch levels and time distances—became a favorite device in Webern's compositional workshop. Some fellow twelve-tone composers have criticized this procedure. It is argued that the twelve-tone technique is by definition canonic, since it requires constant repetition of the chosen row, however modified. Therefore, the application of strict canonic procedure would represent only a kind of duplication of the most basic principle of twelve-tone technique—a rather easy trick. Whatever the merit of this argument, it certainly does not apply to such extraordinary canonic exercises as, for instance, Webern's *Symphony*, Opus 21, of 1928. Although some external aspects (as, for example, the repetition sign after the first section of the first movement, which might cause this section to be taken for an exposition in the classical scheme) suggest the traditional character of a symphony, the structural articulation of the work really relies on constant, very elaborate canonic imitations; these form a chain of shorter and longer models which, by virtue of their being derived from the inverted and retrograde forms of the basic tone row, can be tossed back and forth like spherical objects, and actually are used in such ways. The accuracy and elegance with which the reversibility of these models is worked out emanate a peculiar fascination, seeming to suggest a mysterious possibility for circumventing the one-way direction of time. Undoubtedly this is one of the most prophetic aspects of Webern's music. Here are the roots of the later concept of serialism.

The tendency that is announced in the *Symphony* becomes even clearer in the subsequent works, such as the *Concerto* (Opus 24), and above all in the *Variations for Piano* (Opus 27) of 1936. One might say that the composer is no longer concerned with finding ways to register most faithfully and passionately the emotions of man; rather, he withdraws more and more into the detached, cool, miraculous, and exciting world of the musical patterns, where the abstract spirit of music seems to have its own enigmatic life, sufficient unto itself. What we will notice immediately is a further thinning out of texture. In many places the musical flow is reduced to the tenuous strand of a single tone line. But on closer inspection we will notice a formidable structural discipline, such as has hardly been known in music since the late Middle Ages and Bach's *Art of the Fugue*. In the first place, Webern's twelve-tone rows are always so constructed that various parts of the series are mutually symmetrical; these segments are related to each other as inversion, retrogression, and the like. These correspondences are exploited in the compositions in order to create a network of cross references and continuous local symmetries that are marvelous gems of constructive perfection, elegance, simplicity, and fantastic complexity, all at the same time. The second, very short and very rapid movement of the *Variations for Piano* is one of these amazing specimens: fierce and brittle, intense like a rocket, compact and integrated like a Chinese puzzle.

The next to the last of Webern's works is also a set of *Variations,* in which, however, he again uses the full orchestra (Opus 30). The texture of this work is of course meatier than that of the preceding piano work, but it is again very compact, terse, and—in spite of its intricate serial construction—of extreme simplicity. In a letter of May 26, 1941, to the Austrian poetess, Hildegard Jone, many of whose precious metaphysical verses Webern set to music, he comments on the *Variations:*

> Imagine: there are six tones given, in a *Gestalt* [shape] determined through their order of succession and rhythm, and what comes now is nothing but time-and-again this same shape. Of course in perpetual metamorphosis. . . . This shape now becomes the theme followed by six variations. The theme itself, however, is already nothing but variations, metamorphoses of this first shape. As a unit it is the point of origin for further variations. But this theme with its six variations finally produces formally a structure. . . . Thus, although I have called the piece "Variations," they are welded into a new unity. So many metamorphoses of the first shape produce the theme. This, as a new unit, in turn undergoes as many metamorphoses; these, welded into a new unity, make up the form of the whole.[1]

And, to elucidate his idea further, he quotes Goethe, who says about the *Urphänomen* (the primordial phenomenon) that it is

[1] Anton Webern, *Briefe an Hildegard Jone und Josef Humplik,* ed. Josef Polnauer (Vienna: Universal Edition, 1959), p. 47.

ideal—as the ultimate recognizable;
real—as the recognized;
symbolical—because it comprises all possible cases;
identical with all cases.[2]

Many times Webern has referred to Goethe's philosophy of nature as it is formulated in the *Farbenlehre* and in the treatises on the *Urpflanze* (the primordial plant) and the *os intermaxillare* (the intermediate jawbone). Goethe's viewpoint, indeed, expresses the core of Webern's artistic philosophy: the idea of total integration, unity in multiplicity.

A more technical explanation of the compositional procedure applied in the *Variations* is stated by Webern in a letter to Willi Reich, in Switzerland:

> Everything in this piece is derived from the two ideas stated in the first two measures by the double bass and oboe. The second form of the idea is in retrograde: the second two tones are the retrograde movement of the first two, but are doubled in rhythmic length. Then the trombone states the first form of the double bass, but in half notes. That is how I construct my row, with these three groups of four tones each, in the bass, oboe, trombone.
>
> The motivic development uses much more retrograde motion with augmentation and diminution. . . . By changing the center of gravitation within the two row-forms by augmentation and diminution, the character and meter of the piece is constantly changing. . . . The entire development of the piece is already present in the row of the first few bars: Preformed.[3]

The *Variations for Orchestra*, Opus 30, were written in 1940 and were performed for the first time in 1943 at Winterthur, Switzerland. Webern went there to hear them, and this was the last time he heard any of his music played in public. His isolation had become more severe than ever. For a time he had nourished some vague, utterly fantastic, and unrealistic hopes that the Nazi

[2] Quoted in *ibid.*

[3] See letter to Willi Reich, May 3, 1941, quoted in Walter Kolneder, *Anton Webern: Einführung in Werk und Stil* (Rodenkirchen am Rhein: P. J. Tonger, 1961), p. 140.

regime in Austria might mean a change of attitude toward his music. Such hopes, induced perhaps by a certain bitterness toward the hostile indifference of his countrymen toward his music thus far, quickly vanished into nothingness. The previous rulers had not cared whether his music was played or not—although they preferred that it not be played. The new rulers diligently saw to it that it was *never* played. When increasing air raids made life in Vienna more precarious, Webern withdrew to the village of Mittersill, tucked away in the heart of the Austrian Alps, where relatives of his owned a house. At the end of the war, while Mittersill and the whole Salzburg region were occupied by the American army, Webern was working supposedly on a concerto (actually a third cantata), unconscious of the fact that he had become the prophet of a new movement in musical composition that, within a few years, would engulf the younger generation everywhere. Five months after the termination of hostilities, Anton von Webern was shot to death by an American soldier.[4]

The term "preformed," which Webern uses in his comments on the orchestral *Variations*, is the most important clue to his influence on further developments in musical composition and theory. Thus far, in the twelve-tone technique, it had been only the order of pitches that was prearranged, namely, in accordance with the serial pattern of the tone row. But in Webern's late works one

[4] The circumstances of this tragedy were fully brought to light through the diligent research of Dr. Hans Moldenhauer and were published in his carefully documented book on this fearful incident (see Selected Bibliography).

Had the tragedy of 1945 not occurred, it would be entirely possible that Webern, at the threshold of his eightieth year, would have come to Seattle to witness the triumph of his genius at the festival in his honor. He was not much of a traveler. He liked to go to London once in a while, because he found the work with the excellent orchestra of the BBC particularly congenial. But the surroundings of England remained as foreign to him as did those of Spain, where he was distinctly unhappy when he came to the International Festival of Contemporary Music in Barcelona in 1936. He felt at ease only in the atmosphere of Austria, and really at home in its high mountains, to which he made frequent, though curiously hurried, excursions.

may observe a gradual extension of the principle of premeditated serial arrangements into other aspects of the music. There are rhythmic patterns that reappear in the course of the musical process, not repeated merely to promote the identification of motives or themes (and thus to articulate the over-all form of the composition, as was the case in older music), but reiterated according to a more abstract organizational plan, in order to create local structures of intricate symmetry in coordination with the tone patterns. When Webern in the statement quoted above speaks of his particular use of augmentation and diminution by which the center of gravity is shifted so that the metric picture of the music constantly changes, he hints at concepts of musical organization that only later were completely understood and formulated. The rapid short movement of the *Piano Variations* is a very advanced example of these new ideas. Here every pitch is, so to speak, frozen in its octave register and does not occur in any other. The rhythmic values are equally closely identified with certain configurations of tones, and even in the distribution of the dynamic levels a similar plan may be detected.

Complete serial organization of the all-important dimension of time has become the preoccupation of those composers, young or older, who have chosen Webern's work as a point of departure for their own efforts. These developments I discuss in more detail in "New Dimensions of Music," later in this volume.

JAMES BEALE

Webern's Musical Estate

The Moldenhauer Archive, besides the great wealth of manuscripts, letters, and documents bearing upon contemporary music in general which it contains, is by now well known as one of the most important repositories of Weberniana. It is the purpose of this report to deal briefly with Webern's musical estate as represented in the Archive, consisting of: a number of early compositions predating the *Passacaglia for Orchestra*, Opus 1; sketchbooks; and pianoforte versions of Opera 13, 14, and 29.

Webern's last notebook,[1] begun March 10, 1943, offers us insight into the composer's working procedure. The notebook contains forty-one pages, the first thirty-two of which are the sketches for the second and third movements of the *Cantata*, Opus 31. Webern begins by dividing the poem into small sections; he then makes several versions of the first section, polishing and repolishing before proceeding to the second section, and then to the third, and so on.

Usually the first sketch of each section is close to the published version, subsequent sketches primarily involving changes in rhythm or in the register of notes. Webern seems to have postponed to the last moment such decisions as whether certain figures should, for example, ascend a major third or descend a minor sixth. Even the final sketch often differs from the published score

[1] See "A Webern Archive in America."

in this respect. In the case of the second movement of the *Cantata*, Opus 31, Webern sketched the movement as beginning in 2/4 meter; yet the published version begins in 2/2. (There are also sketches of the first section of this movement beginning in 1/4 and 1/2 meters.)

In general, Webern condenses the instrumental parts onto three staves as he sketches forward, indicating instrumentation from time to time in colored pencil.

Pages 33 and 34 of the notebook contain an abandoned movement—readily identified by the tone row—which would have been part of the *Cantata*, Opus 31. On page 35, Webern planned a concerto, writing the three-movement plan at the top of page 35: "Sonate—Adagio—Rondo." When the page is turned, however, words appear. These words have been identified as belonging to the poem cycle *Lumen* by Hildegard Jone. Subsequently, correspondence between Dr. Moldenhauer and Hildegard Jone has confirmed that Webern was indeed planning a third cantata at the time of his death.

The tone row of this cantata would have had a symmetry typical of the last period (Example 1).

Example 1. Webern, tone row from sketches for a third cantata

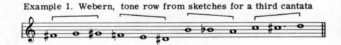

In the remaining five pages of the notebook, Webern works on the setting of the first eight words of the poem:

Das Sonnenlicht spricht:
Aufgeht der Vorhang der Nacht! . . .

The last choral setting in the sketchbook is noteworthy for its parallelism, recalling the choral piece *Entflieht auf leichten Kähnen*, Opus 2 (Example 2).

Thus Webern might have closed the circle, combining the tech-

Example 2. Webern, choral setting from the last sketchbook

Copyright 1961 Hans Moldenhauer

nique of his last choral works with something of the texture and feeling of his earliest. It cannot be assumed that this passage is in its final form, however, for on the last page the composer, in his constant search for perfection, embarks upon still another version of the opening—a version that breaks off after four measures.

The discovery of Webern autographs of early works predating Opus 1 has naturally aroused great interest. The manuscripts in question, all contained in the Moldenhauer Archive, are as follows:

Fourteen songs (1899-1904)
A ballad for voice and orchestra, *Siegfrieds Schwert* (1903)
An idyll for large orchestra, *Im Sommerwind* (1904)
Langsamer Satz for string quartet (1905)
String Quartet (1905)
Quintet for string quartet and piano (1906)
Five *Dehmel Lieder* (1906-8).

The fourteen[2] songs (they are separate songs) are settings of texts that range through Avenarius, Dehmel, Goethe, Nietzsche, Falke, Greif, Weigand, Claudius, and Liliencron. The musical influences are both first-rate and ordinary. Among the first-rate

[2] A fifteenth early song, "Liebeslied," was abandoned by the composer. Its two and one half lines are virtually illegible.

influences immediately apparent is that of Hugo Wolf. From Wolf, Webern acquires a directness and succinctness of expression that is ever after to remain characteristic of his music. Occasionally there is a thematic link between the two composers, as can be seen by comparing the opening of Webern's "Aufblick" with Wolf's "Lebe Wohl" (Example 3).

Example 3. (a) Wolf, Lebe wohl; (b) Webern, Aufblick

Sometimes there are surprising stylistic turns. The song "Blumengruss," on the poem by Goethe, begins with a phrase (Example 4) that might have been written by a composer as remote from Webern's circle as Gabriel Fauré.

Example 4. Webern, Blumengruss

There are also places in the earliest songs where Webern has a disconcerting way of sounding like his English contemporary, John Ireland. Their common source is to be found among the secondary composers at the turn of the century, in a style that features overmuch the tonic triad with the fifth in the soprano, the progression I—V^7—I over a tonic pedal, and tentative experiments with the dominant ninth and diatonic seventh chords. It is a style somewhat "modernized" in later years by Ireland and Cyril Scott, whereas Webern soon began to pursue his independent course.

It is interesting that Webern, from the first, takes a rigorous attitude toward form. Among these fourteen songs not one is strophic, nor does any fall back upon the A-B-A formula of the three-part song form. Each song unfolds through to its conclusion, although once in a great while the opening may be recalled in the piano accompaniment in a final phrase after the voice part is completed. The more poignant moments in the songs are brought about, not so much through the use of complex "advanced" chords, but rather by using ordinary chords in novel ways, or by juxtaposing distantly related keys.

By contrast, *Siegfrieds Schwert* (1903), a ballad for voice and orchestra, on the poem by Friedrich Uhland, is disappointing. One might suppose from the title that the work would be very Wagnerian in style, but this is not the case at all. If anything, it has a Handelian flavor, with something of the feeling and pace of the celebrated "Harmonious Blacksmith" variations. The harmony is very plain, almost entirely triadic, with only an occasional diatonic seventh chord. Even at the cadences the dominant triad is preferred to the dominant seventh chord. In addition, it is extremely homophonic, to the point where one wonders if it might not have been merely a harmony exercise orchestrated for the experience of score making. There are several blunders in the score—transpositions forgotten, poor placement of some instruments in *tutti* passages, and the like. At times, Webern remembers that the string bass sounds an octave lower than written; at other times, it is apparent that he has forgotten. All things considered, one is forced to admit that *Siegfrieds Schwert* will remain a manuscript of historical interest only.

The instrumental music of 1904-6 is quite another matter. By this time Webern, under the guidance of Schoenberg, had acquired a considerable mastery of the advanced techniques of the time. The symphonic poem *Im Sommerwind* (1904), which the composer subtitles "An Idyll for Orchestra," is inspired by a poem of the same title by the German poet Bruno Wille (1860-1928)—a poem that apparently touched Webern for its deep love of nature.

In the early part of this tone poem each section unfolds a new theme, while motifs from previous sections appear as countermelodies or countermelodic fragments. Occasionally these returning motifs gain equality or even predominance over the theme of the section. In the latter part of the work, these motifs continue to unfold and develop against one another in perpetual development, an indication of how rapidly Webern was absorbing Schoenberg's influence at this time. The motifs that Schoenberg combines in a work such as *Pelleas und Melisande* tend to be more complex and improvisatory than the more square-cut ones of Webern in *Im Sommerwind*. Webern's melodic thrusts are often of one or two measures' duration, not unlike the "breathing" of the "Liebestod" in *Tristan und Isolde*.

Harmonically, *Im Sommerwind* shows that Webern has thoroughly absorbed the vocabulary of Richard Strauss, even sharing his predilection for *forte* 6/4 chords at heroic moments in the score. Indeed, this work is the most frankly Wagnerian-Straussian of all Webern's *opera*.

The following orchestral reduction (Example 5), beginning two measures after cue 9, shows an example of the way in which Webern combined various motives in a *tutti* passage. (The motives are lettered in the order in which they appear in this excerpt, and not in the order of appearance in the work as a whole.)

After the world première[3] of *Im Sommerwind*, one critic spoke

[3] In Seattle, May 25, 1962, by the Philadelphia Orchestra, Eugene Ormandy, conductor.

Example 5. Webern, Im Sommerwind

of certain silences that foreshadow Webern's later style. Actually, these silences may not be flights of genius at all, but merely incomplete places in the score, of which there may be as many as five. First, these silences do not have the same kind of tension as do the "silent notes" of Opus 5 and after. Second, Webern is careful to put rests in all parts on other pages. Since these possibly unfinished places occur only briefly in link passages, the over-all sweep of the piece is not destroyed. In addition, the score has many beautiful passages, notably the beginning and ending with its shimmering D-major chord played by divided strings.

The instrumentation of *Im Sommerwind* is three flutes, two

oboes, English horn, four clarinets, two bassoons, six horns, two trumpets, two harps, timpani, triangle, cymbals, and strings. The omission of trombones and the inclusion of six horns is noteworthy.

Webern composed two works for string quartet in 1905: a *Quartet* in one movement, as well as a separate *Langsamer Satz.* Of the two works, the *Langsamer Satz* seems disarmingly conventional in its harmony, form, and emotional content. Although the two works were completed only a few weeks apart, the *Langsamer Satz* is much less venturesome, and at times perhaps almost sugary in its content. Suffice it to say that Webern applies the same rigorous attention to technical detail that characterizes his more "progressive" pieces. Special interest is focused both upon contrapuntal thematic development and upon the possibilities of unusual quartet texture.

The first two notes of the piece are already unusual. Although the first section is of itself an A-B-A in E-flat major, the two opening notes make a feint toward C minor (Example 6). The re-

Example 6. Webern, Langsamer Satz

sulting E-flat major triad with the added sixth may well have been suggested to Webern by the beginning of Schoenberg's *Gurrelieder.* Although the texture of the two openings is quite different, the same chord is used in the same key. In the *Langsamer Satz* the chord lends a surprising tonal ambiguity to the piece—an ambiguity strengthened by the fact that the stormier second section is in G minor. The listener hearing the piece for the first time cannot be absolutely certain which way the tonality will resolve.

After the stormier second section, the third section seems all the more peaceful; the serene beauty of its opening phrase should lay at rest the doubts of those who might question whether Webern was ever capable of writing "melody" in the more conventional sense (Example 7). The theme in Example 7 is presented

Example 7. Webern, Langsamer Satz

in C major, and then in A-flat major, after which the first section returns, followed by a coda that ends the piece in E-flat major.

As the opening theme returns several times throughout the piece, Webern finds several ways of accompanying the theme with the other three instruments. Toward the end, he uses varied combinations of plucked and muted sounds as accompaniment texture, showing early his interest in the less conventional string sounds. It should be emphasized that the use of such devices here is only decorative, and not yet functional, as it was to become in Opera 5 and 9.

The *String Quartet*, completed August 25, 1905, is quite different in style. The *Quartet* is in one movement, in the same sense that Schoenberg's *Verklärte Nacht* is in one movement—it is a large piece in several sections, comparable in musical experience to a work of many movements. The harmony is a great deal more subtle than that of either the *Langsamer Satz* or *Im Sommerwind*, and there are long sections in which it is difficult to put one's finger on a precise key center. On the other hand, there are sections of the *Quartet* that are very firmly in a tonality, again reminiscent of *Verklärte Nacht,* which also unfolds in a rapidly fluctuating tonality at times, only to land foursquare in a definitive key at other times.

The opening section of the Webern *Quartet* is based on a three-note motive (Example 8). The first section unfolds from this three-

Example 8. Webern, String Quartet (1905)

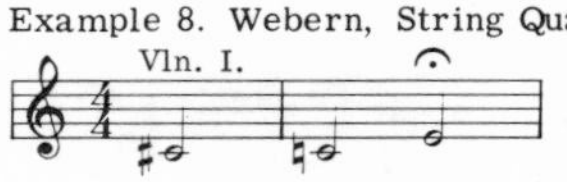

note motive in a constant tonal flux. The chords Webern uses here fall into the following color types: (1) the chord of the raised fifth, either in its triadic or seventh-chord form (occurs 20 times); (2) the dominant seventh with flatted fifth—the so-called "French-sixth" sound (occurs 14 times); (3) secondary seventh-chord sounds not resolving in relation to a key center, but moving smoothly to one of the chords in categories 1 or 2 (occurs 8 times); (4) one example each of a dominant-seventh-chord sound and a dominant-ninth-chord sound. This section, then, is quite remarkable harmonically in that it unfolds as if in a harmonic system of its own, using a relatively small number of particular chord sounds.

It is here for the first time in Webern's music that we find the silences and *sotto voce* remarks typical of his later works: the four-part texture is interrupted occasionally to present the three-note motive *pizzicato* and *pianissimo* on one instrument (Example 9).

After this section, which is introductory in character, a longer theme takes the center of the stage (Example 10). The melodic ancestor of this theme is found in *Verklärte Nacht,* seven measures after cue F (Example 11). The themes of both examples include a quintuplet figure, followed by the upward skip of a

Example 9. Webern, String Quartet (1905)

Example 10. Webern, String Quartet (1905)

Example 11. Schoenberg, Verklärte Nacht

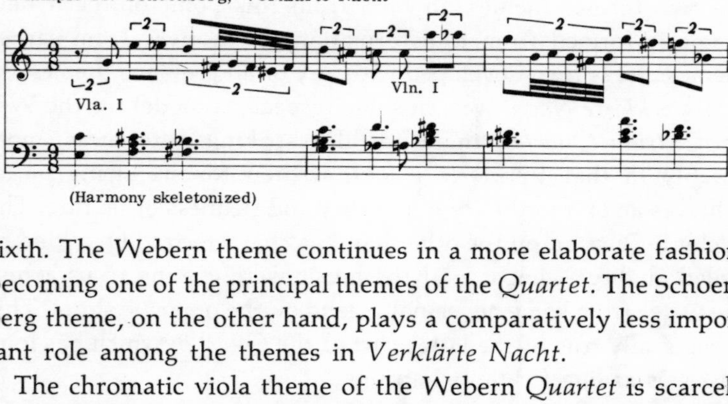

sixth. The Webern theme continues in a more elaborate fashion, becoming one of the principal themes of the *Quartet*. The Schoenberg theme, on the other hand, plays a comparatively less important role among the themes in *Verklärte Nacht*.

The chromatic viola theme of the Webern *Quartet* is scarcely exposed before the three-note motive of the first section returns, and the two ideas are developed together in a highly contrapuntal fashion. It is not until the piece is some three minutes along that a key signature appears and the music settles for the first time around a key center (E major), while introducing a third theme

(Example 12). This theme has the elements of the other two themes in it; the rise of a third in the three-note motive is echoed here by the fall of a third, and the four chromatic notes that follow form the inversion of four similar notes from the theme shown in Example 10.

Example 12. Webern, String Quartet (1905)

The third section continues with the immediate development of this new theme, interwoven with the continued development of the two former themes. In fact, from this point on, each new theme is formed from transformations of motives from earlier themes and is then developed with any or all previous themes.

If *Verklärte Nacht* was, in some respects, a model for the Webern *String Quartet,* there are also striking differences, most notably in that *Verklärte Nacht,* written for six string parts, achieves an extraordinary luminosity and richness of texture. The Webern *Quartet,* on the other hand, is characterized by a kind of veiled quality—almost as if the music were coming to us across the water from some never-never land on the opposite shore. This is especially true of the latter part of the *Quartet,* which has long passages calling for muted strings.

The over-all form of the *Quartet* falls into two parts marked by similar closing-theme material at the end of each part; to this is added a coda, itself containing three distinct smaller sections, the last of which returns to the three-note figure of the beginning (although continuing to the final cadence with different music).

That Webern was never far from words, even when writing for instruments, is clear from the quotation which he inscribed on the title page of this *Quartet:*

> The sense of triumph that prevailed within my spirit I cannot write, nor tell; it can with naught be compared, save only where in the midst of death, life is born, like unto the resurrection of the dead. In this light did my mind forthwith penetrate all things; and in all living creatures, even in weeds and grass, did perceive God, who He is, and how He is, and what be His will.

The words are by the Renaissance mystic, Jacob Böhme (1575-1624); they give us some feeling of the seriousness and dedication with which Webern approached each new composition.

The *Quintet* for piano and string quartet (1907) is the one previously known work of the early compositions, since it was published in 1953.[4] Again we find a work of one large movement, falling more nearly into a sonata-form pattern than the previous *Quartet*. Webern continues his exploration of advanced harmonies and fluctuating tonalities, although the tonality is made clear at certain critical places in the form. The *Quintet* plainly begins and ends in C major, for example. The interest in special effects for stringed instruments is again evident in the places marked *tremolo sul ponticello* at the beginning and end of the development section, although the effects are still more decorative than functional.

Perhaps the most surprising quality of the *Quintet* is the kind of Brahmsian rhetoric with which it is pervaded. It is not the harmony which is reminiscent of Brahms, but rather the sonority and the rhythmic articulation: the three-against-two and three-against-four rhythms, the *bravura* piano writing tending toward thick sonority, and the use of parallel thirds to express lyricism. If there is, however, a specific piece that can be said to have influenced the *Quintet,* that piece is the first movement of the Strauss *Violin Sonata* in E-flat major, Opus 18. Both works fea-

[4] Boelke-Bomart Music Publications, Inc., Hillsdale, New York.

ture, to some extent, the rhythmic figure  , or variants of this rhythm. Both works have an agitated development that calms before the recapitulation, and both main themes return in the piano, beginning on the tonic triad with the third in the soprano.

With the five songs of 1906-8, on poems by Richard Dehmel, we reach the culmination of the early period. In these songs Webern shows complete mastery of the technique of the Viennese school. Brought into a fluent idiom are all the advanced chords of the period: augmented chords, the French-sixth sound, freely inverted ninth chords, and even chords built on the whole-tone scale. Yet the harmony is not as consistently daring as that of the songs of Opera 3 and 4. For example, in the songs of Opera 3 and 4, those that do not end on a single note end on a dissonance. In the *Dehmel Lieder,* three of the songs retreat to the safety of a tonic major triad at the end. Only the last song ends on a dissonance. Despite the use of the same kinds of harmonic materials by Webern, Berg, and Schoenberg, the differences in the musical personalities of the three composers are discernible. Webern's texture, for example, seems almost spidery in comparison to the opulent, heavily vegetated vocabulary of Alban Berg.

The first four of the five *Dehmel Lieder* can be said to be in A-B-A three-part form if a somewhat liberal interpretation is given to the term. This is because Webern has taken the trouble to hide the seams between the three sections. Typically, the first measure of the recapitulation is different from the beginning, and it is not until the second or third measure of the recapitulation that the link to the beginning is made—and even then a change of texture or harmony is not uncommon. Often Webern will leave the repetition quickly, and the remainder of the third section will unfold quite differently from the first. Some might question as to whether this is enough to give the impression of a three-part song form. However, if one studies the poems themselves, invariably these repetitions are found to occur at those moments in the poems at which we would expect a recapitulation to take place, if one were going to take place at all.

The texts of the *Dehmel Lieder* are concerned with the description of landscape, particularly at night, and man's relation to the landscape. It is interesting to note how many of the Dehmel texts are concerned with night, not only in these songs but also in the very early Webern songs which are settings of Dehmel poems. Schoenberg's *Verklärte Nacht* was also inspired by a Dehmel poem. This undoubtedly reflects the expressionists' association of night with darkness, mystery, loneliness, and even, in other circumstances, with horror, the clandestine, and so forth.

The fifth and final song of the set, "Helle Nacht," is an extraordinary example of Webern's concern for contrapuntal design. The song is written in triple counterpoint. If, in the first stanza, we call the voice part *a*, the right hand of the piano part *b*, and the left hand of the piano part *c*, the subsequent stanzas use the permutations shown in the following chart:

	Stanza 1	Stanza 2	Stanza 3
voice	*a*	*b*	*a*
piano, r.h.	*b*	*a*	*c*
piano, l.h.	*c*	*c*	*b*

Although the song is plainly a strophic type, the fact that the voice part is the same for Stanzas 1 and 3, while differing in the middle, gives the song at the same time the feeling of a three-part A-B-A structure.

In addition, there is a brief introduction for the piano (Example 13). This phrase ends with one of Webern's famous sighs—the single chord marked *ppp,* so delicate that one can hardly bear to play it. This phrase returns in a modified form, occasionally with the voice participating, between every two stanzas and also at the end. The phrase is slightly extended in the coda, and the opening figure is itself inverted (Example 14).

It is no exaggeration to say that the *Dehmel Lieder* represent an

Example 13. Webern, Helle Nacht

Example 14. Webern, Helle Nacht

important contribution to song literature. When the early works of Webern were first discovered, there were some who had misgivings about the propriety of bringing forth this music, as if the searching and struggles of the young composer were in some way unsightly. On the contrary, performance has shown most of these works to have an intrinsic artistic merit of their own. Moreover, studying them has enabled us to gain insight into the creative development of Anton von Webern, and thus to achieve greater understanding of his work in its totality.

Portrait photograph of Webern, Stettin, October, 1912
[*Webern Archive*]

Photograph of Webern in his Mödling studio, summer, 1930 [*Webern Archive*]

Manuscript page from *Vorfrühling* (1899), one of Webern's earliest extant compositions. Copyright 1961 and 1965, Carl Fischer, Inc. [*Webern Archive*]

Page 20 of the autograph score of *Im Sommerwind*, idyll for large orchestra (19
Copyright 1962 and 1966, Carl Fischer, Inc. [*Webern Archive*]

Manuscript page from "Helle Nacht" (1908), the last in the cycle of *Five Dehmel Songs*. Copyright 1962 and 1966, Carl Fischer, Inc. [*Webern Archive*]

Arnold Schönberg, meinem Lehrer und Freunde in höchster Liebe

Sechs Stücke

für

grosses Orchester

von

Anton von Webern

op. 4

Meinem lieben Vater

Klagenfurt, April 1913

Im Selbstverlag des Komponisten

Aufführungsrecht vorbehalten.

Title page of an early publication of *Six Pieces for Large Orchestra,* Opus 6, under Webern's own imprint. The work is here designated Opus 4. The copy bears the composer's autograph dedication to his father (1913) [*Webern Archive*]

Mödling bei Wien
Neusiedlerstraße 58

Mein lieber Herr Weiss,

vielen Dank Ihnen und Ihrer lieben Frau für Ihre uns sehr erfreuenden Weihnachts- u. Neujahrswünsche.
Wir erwidern diese auf das Allerherzlichste!
Ihre Anfrage, ob ich „auf drei Monate als Dirigent eines neuen Orchesters" nach New York kommen möchte, hat mich auf das Angenehmste überrascht. Ja, sehr gerne!
Doch, glauben Sie mir, es sind nicht bloß Erwägungen materieller Art, die mich hinüberlocken, sondern vor allem die Hoffnung, drüben eine wahrhaft befriedigende Tätigkeit finden zu können u. der Glaube, dass das, was mir vorschwebt, heute vielleicht einzig nur in Amerika möglich ist.
Nun müssen Sie mir aber ehestens Genaueres berichten; informieren Sie mich über die Art der Stellung möglichst eingehend, bitte.
Um was für ein Orchester handelt es sich?
Was für Konzerte u. wie viele sind geplant?
Wieso käme gerade die Zeit von drei Monaten für meine Tätigkeit in Betracht? Welche Monate? Noch in dieser Saison?
Welche Zukunft könnte die Sache haben?

Erst, wenn ich das Alles weiß, kann ich

Letter from Webern to Adolph Weiss (Mödling, December 26, 1930), placing high hopes on the prospect of coming to America [*Webern Archive*]

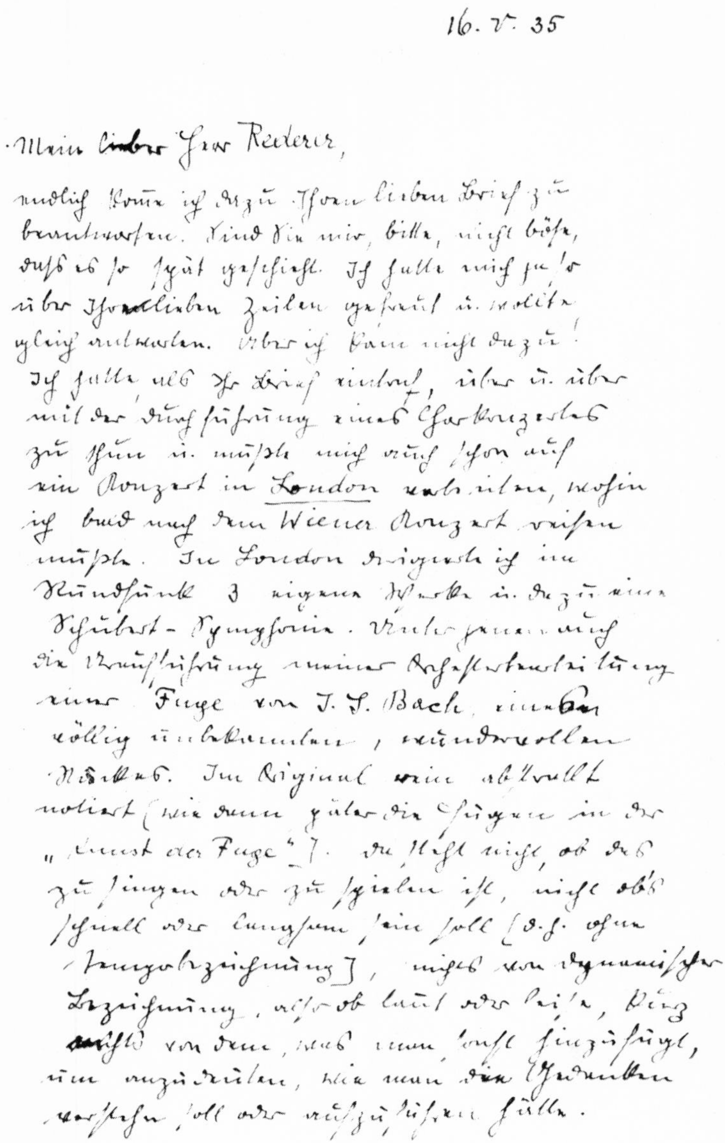
16. V. 35

Mein lieber Herr Rederer,

endlich komme ich dazu Ihren lieben Brief zu beantworten. Sind Sie mir, bitte, nicht böse, daß es so spät geschieht. Ich hatte mich ja so über Ihre lieben Zeilen gefreut u. wollte gleich antworten. Aber ich kam nicht dazu! Ich hatte, als Ihr Brief eintraf, über u. über mit der Aufführung eines Chorkonzertes zu thun u. mußte mich auch schon auf ein Konzert in London vorbereiten, wohin ich bald nach dem Wiener Konzert reisen mußte. In London dirigierte ich im Rundfunk 3 eigene Werke u. dazu eine Schubert-Symphonie. Unter anderem auch die Uraufführung meiner Orchesterbearbeitung einer Fuge von J. S. Bach, eines völlig unbekannten, wundervollen Werkes. Im Original ganz abstrakt notiert (wie denn gerade die Fugen in der „Kunst der Fuge"). Da steht nicht, ob das zu singen oder zu spielen ist, nicht ob's schnell oder langsam sein soll (d. h. ohne Tempobezeichnung), nichts von dynamischer Bezeichnung, also ob laut oder leise, kurz nichts von dem, was man sonst hinzufügt, um anzudeuten, wie man den Gedanken verstehen soll oder auszuführen hätte.

Letter from Webern to Franz Rederer (Maria Enzersdorf, May 16, 1935), commenting on Webern's instrumentation of J. S. Bach's *Ricercar* [*Webern Archive*]

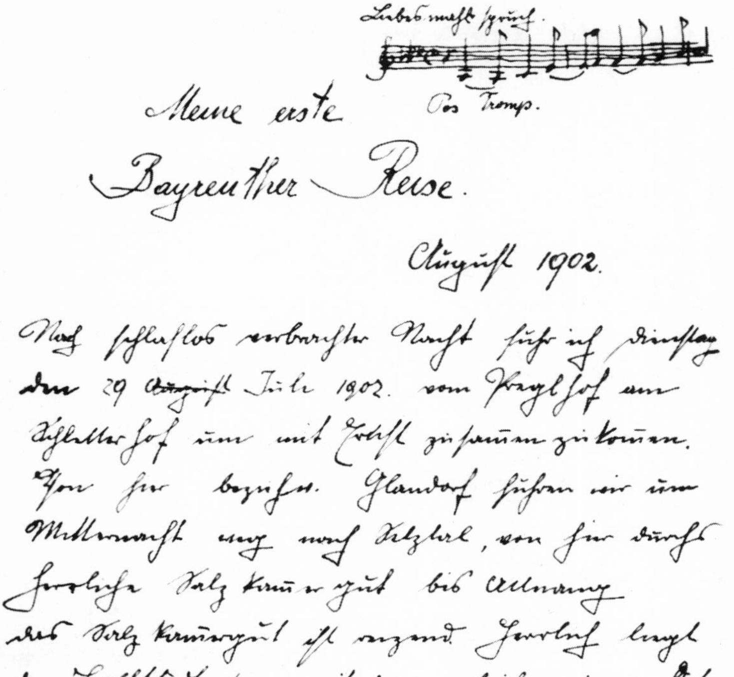

Page from Webern's first diary (Bayreuth pilgrimage, 1902), with the Love Feast motive (*Liebesmahlspruch*) from *Parsifal* [*Webern Archive*]

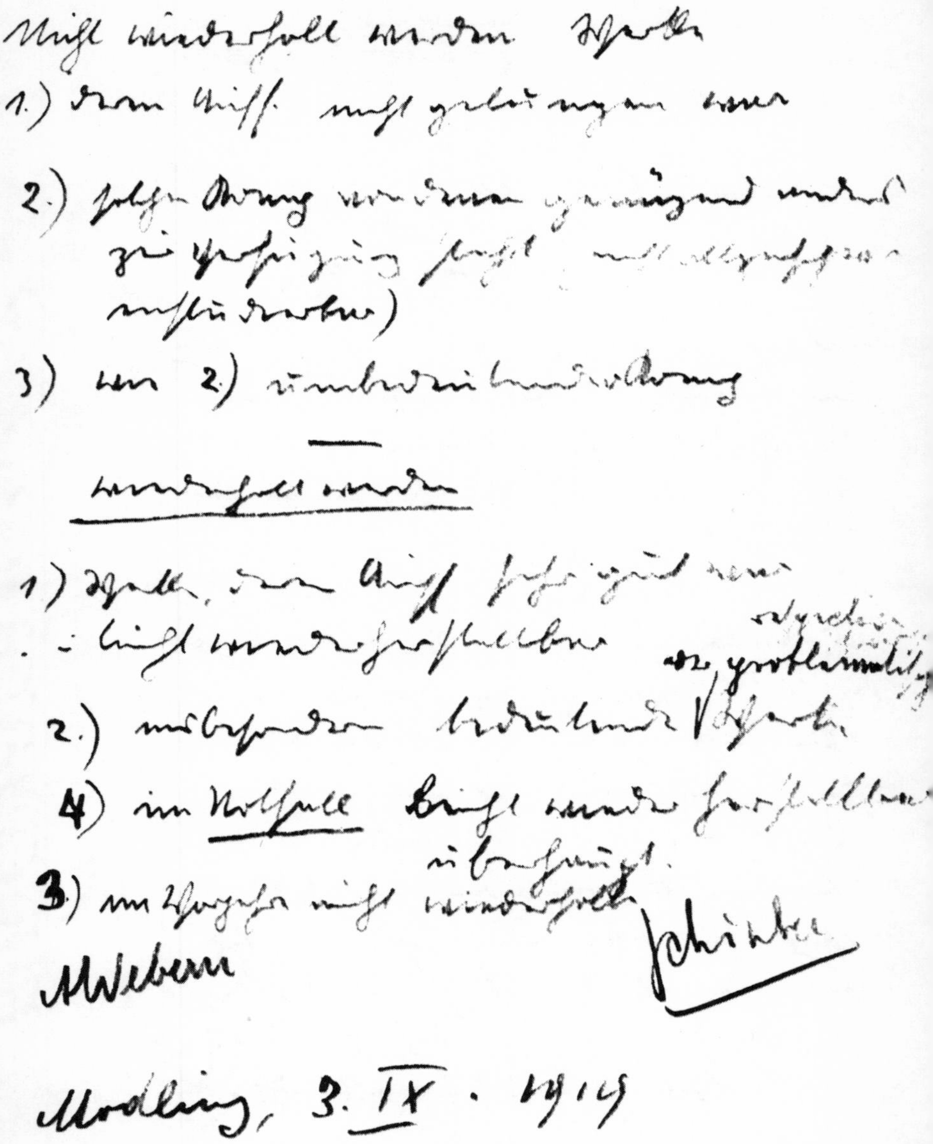

Excerpt from a diary: statement of policy drawn for the Verein für musikalisch Privataufführungen, cosigned by Webern and Schoenberg (Mödling, September . 1919) [*Webern Archive*]

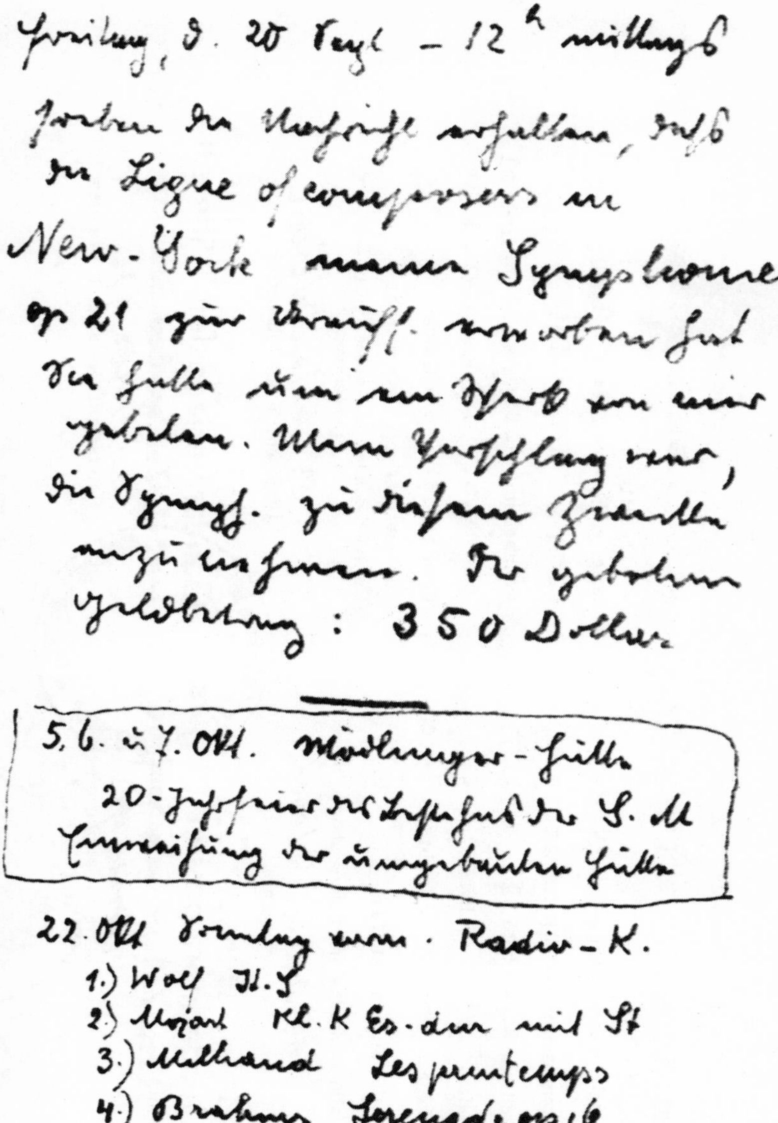

Freitag, d. 20 Sept – 12h mittags

Soeben die Nachricht erhalten, daß die League of composers in New-York meine Symphonie op 21 zur Uraufführ. erworben hat. [illegible] um ein Werk von mir gebeten. Mein Vorschlag war, die Symph. zu diesem Zwecke anzunehmen. Der gebotene Geldbetrag: 350 Dollar

5, 6. u. 7. Okt. Mödlinger-Halle
20-Jahrfeier des Bestehens der S. M
[illegible] der umgebauten Halle

22. Okt Sonntag vorm. Radio-K.
1.) Wolf It. S
2.) Mozart Kl. K Es-dur mit St
3.) Milhaud Les printemps
4.) Brahms Serenade op 16

Page from Webern's last diary (1929) [*Webern Archive*]

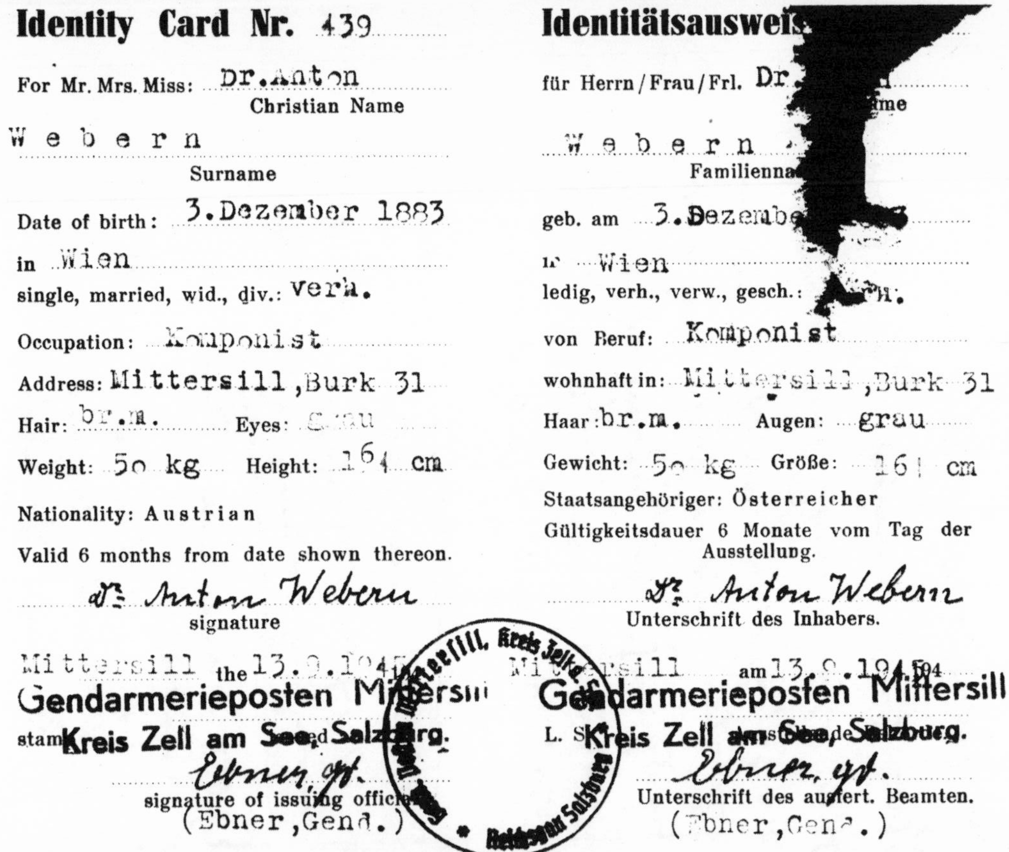
Identity Card Nr. 439

For Mr. Mrs. Miss: Dr. Anton
Christian Name

W e b e r n
Surname

Date of birth: 3. Dezember 1883

in Wien

single, married, wid., div.: verh.

Occupation: Komponist

Address: Mittersill, Burk 31

Hair: br. m. Eyes: grau

Weight: 50 kg Height: 164 cm

Nationality: Austrian

Valid 6 months from date shown thereon.

Dr. Anton Webern
signature

Mittersill the 13.9.1945

Gendarmerieposten Mittersill
Kreis Zell am See, Salzburg.

Ebner, gr.
signature of issuing officer
(Ebner, Gend.)

Identitätsausweis

für Herrn/Frau/Frl. Dr.
...me

W e b e r n
Familienna...

geb. am 3. Dezembe...

in Wien

ledig, verh., verw., gesch.: ...h.

von Beruf: Komponist

wohnhaft in: Mittersill, Burk 31

Haar: br. m. Augen: grau

Gewicht: 50 kg Größe: 164 cm

Staatsangehöriger: Österreicher

Gültigkeitsdauer 6 Monate vom Tag der Ausstellung.

Dr. Anton Webern
Unterschrift des Inhabers.

Mittersill am 13.9.1945

Gendarmerieposten Mittersill
Kreis Zell am See, Salzburg.

Ebner, gr.
Unterschrift des ausfert. Beamten.
(Ebner, Gend.)

Identity card issued two days before Webern's death. The tear in the document presumably resulted from a bullet [*Webern Archive*].

PAUL A. PISK

Webern's Early Orchestral Works

Until recently, the first generally known work by Anton von Webern was his *Passacaglia for Orchestra,* Opus 1. With Alban Berg the situation was much the same, for his first opus number was assigned to the *Piano Sonata.* Both composers, however, had written earlier works which have been discovered much later. In Webern's case, besides the early songs and chamber music, there were two compositions for orchestra. The first of these, *Siegfrieds Schwert* (Siegfried's Sword), for solo voice and orchestra, was written in September, 1903. The second, *Im Sommerwind: Idylle für grosses Orchester* (Summer Wind: Idyll for Large Orchestra), one year later. The sketch was completed on August 5, and the full score on September 16, 1904. Preglhof, a country estate in Carinthia owned by Webern's family, where the young composer used to spend his vacations, is indicated as the place where he finished both works.

The first piece shows definite signs of being a student essay. Simple folklike melodies in square sections, very plain harmonies, and stereotype orchestration—all these reveal Webern as grappling with craftsmanship. And yet even in this attempt innate musical ability and a feeling for structural balance can be observed.

The artistic development between *Siegfrieds Schwert* and *Im Sommerwind* is amazing. It is true that in the second work we still find strong influences of the later Romanticists. Style elements of Wagner, Liszt, and perhaps also Richard Strauss can be traced in the score. Already present, however, are a complete command of the technique of motivic development, an acute sense of formal balance, a masterful use of harmonic means, and a personal treatment of the orchestra. Furthermore, the problem of writing program music based on a poem and at the same time satisfying the requirements of absolute musical form is successfully solved.

The poem that furnished the background for Webern's composition is by Bruno Wille (1860-1928). This North German author is better known today as a religious and social philosopher than as a novelist and lyricist. He founded the Freie Volksbühne (Free Theater Guild) in Berlin, as well as a "Free University," and also edited a periodical, *The Free-Thinker.* Despite his liberal, even socialistic, leanings, he was never active in politics. As a matter of fact, he withdrew from urban civilization and looked for consolation and purification through close association with nature. The village of Friedrichshagen, on a lake east of Berlin, was his abode, as it was also of Bölsche and the brothers Hart, then prominent figures in German literature. Even such famous writers as Gerhard Hauptmann came to visit these Friedrichshagen lyricists. The poem *Im Sommerwind* was an interpolation into an autobiographical novel by Wille, *Offenbarungen des Wacholderbaums* ("Revelations of a Juniper Tree"), written in 1895 and published in 1901. Webern must have read this novel, because Wille's volume of poetry, *Der heilige Hain* ("The Sacred Grove"), in which we find the poem today, was not published until 1908.

Im Sommerwind, written in free verse without rhymes, consists of seven large sections of varying lengths, the shortest being ten lines and the longest twenty lines. The descriptive element prevails throughout, but the various sections differ in mood and intensity, so that there is a noticeable structural organization and a building up of climaxes. The first section depicts a typical North German landscape, aglow in the bright colors of the summer.

The starting of a breeze (Section 2) intensifies the impression made by the colorful scenery upon the poet. A solemn, almost hymnlike adoration of the flowers and meadows constitutes the third section, while the next two sections dwell upon the interplay of light, clouds, and wind. The intensity of motion has increased, but the menacing element of a storm is absent. Only the "jubilant, organlike" roar of the wind enlivens the picture. The wind then dies down, and contemplative serenity is restored. The last two sections describe the effect of this observation of nature upon the human personality. The poet has been delivered from the anxieties of the city, and has found peace and wisdom in the beauties of his beloved summer fields.

Today, Wille's imagery seems evanescent, his metaphors commonplace.[1] But it is easy to understand why Webern was attracted to this poem; he was always an ardent lover of the outdoors and drew his spiritual inspiration from his close contact with nature. In his approach to the poem, he emphasized the differences of the sections. Some are closely knit and concise ones; others are more traditional and aphoristic. Keys, meters, and tempos vary, but unity is achieved by the use of the same thematic material and an over-all formal organization. The symphonic idyll can be considered a ring form with an extended center section. This part, which contains the combinations of several motives, can also be called a development. The organization as a loose sonata form with abridged recapitulation then emerges. A detailed discussion of this analysis, aided by a chart of motives, follows.

The introduction (bars 1-20), above an extended pedal on D, contains in bars 11-12 in the violas the first principal motive (1). Its components, the ascending and descending chromatic notes

[1] Examples: ". . . look, / How Mistress Sun / Coquettishly spreads out her fan / Of silver-silken rays; / Her dazzling limbs / Again emerge / From out their snowy cloud-dress"; "Infinite quiet / In the all-embracing vault of heaven!"

Webern, Im Sommerwind, motive chart

(x, x') and the diatonic falling second (y), are the building material for several later motives. After a dissolution and modulation to F major, the next subsection (bars 21-39) introduces the second main motive (2), which is related to the previous one and is most important. It appears in the violins, imitated by the cellos and violas adorned by supporting lines. Soon this aggregate dissolves also, rounding off the musical equivalent of the first stanza of the poem. Motive 3 ("gaily") obviously marks the starting of the breeze. A short transition with motivic fragments (bars 40-43) leads to the next fast part (bars 44-71). Here motives 3 and 2 (the latter in a rhythmic transformation 2a) are combined. The texture is dense in the beginning; the keys change often (A—E flat—C—G—etc.); but later density and motion decrease. At the end a descending chromatic line (4) is prominent. Immediately before a caesura, the reuse of the aphoristic material of the first transition proves that economy of means and logical distribution of the material were already necessities for the composer. The musical image of this part corresponds with the verbal description of the sunny world, the beginning of the motion of the wind, and the increasing subjective participation of the observer.

Completely different is the ensuing solemn section (bars 72-102; see motive 5), referring to the exalted verses of the third section of the poem on the beauty of the landscape. The ascending chromaticism in the melody refers back to motive 1, but the luscious harmonization in triads in mediant relation (F—A flat—A—D) alters the character. At its second appearance this motive is changed in direction and harmony, and it continues into a descending diatonic line which becomes independent as motive 6. It is inverted right away (6a) and is later used in several rhythmic transformations, like motive 2, which is here changed to 2b in new disguise. Motive 4 also appears in a slightly different version (4a), played in unison by the full orchestra. Motivic-combination counterpoint is fully developed in this section, which suddenly breaks off and reverts to single motives and fragments, already known from earlier transitional elements. Quotations of the "wind" motive (3) are especially apropos.

The "soaring" fast central portion of the idyll (bars 107-61), corresponding with the climactic fourth and fifth stanzas of the poem, indicates the full impact of the summer wind. There are not only the sixteenth-note motive (7) and a new combination of the chromatic and diatonic elements of motives 1 and 2, but also variegated appearances of 2a, 3, and 6b, in more or less exact form, but in different keys (A—C—E flat). This is the most complicated, intricate section of the entire work, emphasizing the melodic and harmonic possibilities of the thematic material in full orchestration. It is matched only by its modified return after a transition (bars 141-61) and a transparent, codalike section (bars 162-75). This transition brings back the wind motive complete and in form 3a, the chromatic line 4, and fragments from 2. Here Webern's extreme sensitivity to delicate sound colors (three solo violins, *tremolo sul ponticello*) is pointing to the future.

In the sixth stanza of the poem, the poet recalls the depression and confusion of city life and reflects that the "stifling old oppression" has now yielded, been submerged; the contemplation of nature has brought a sense of utter peace and serenity. It is not difficult to find parallels to these thoughts in the music. Over an extended chordal harmony in the horns and a slowly oscillating clarinet figure, motive 3b sounds in the oboe—tender and very quiet, but still recognizable in relation to the "wind" motive. This section, like the mind of the poet, comes to a complete rest. The effect is much like that of a coda.

Once more the return of the wind, described in the second half of the poem's sixth section, leads to a modified reprise of the development section (bars 176-206). The jubilant tone and the climax are similar to those of the previous appearance in the central portion; the motives are also alike. They return, however, in different meter and shape. Motive 6b is combined with 3b; the "soaring" motive (7) is heard, as well as the "wind" motives 3 and 3b, and the chromatic line 4, this time intoned broadly, in the strongest dynamics and without a diminishing close. The following very slow transition (bars 207-18) uses the same material as the codalike portion, only fragmented. Motives 4, 3b, even the clarinet figure (for one bar), and parts of 1 are readily recognized.

The music corresponding with the final stanza of the poem is very quiet and serene. In the first part (bars 219-32), the mood of the solemn section (bars 72 ff.) is recaptured. Motive 6 (in imitations) dominates; a part of 3b joins it, and motive 2a, slightly changed in rhythm, is played in the second violins. This motive ascends into the high register (bars 233-39), followed by the soft intonation of 3b in the English horn, and a tender reminiscence of the "wind" motive (3) in the flute. Motive 1 (bars 240-55), again over a pedal point and in D, brings the work to a close. Once more, a dreamlike repeat of motive 3b in the clarinet makes us conscious of the mystery of the poet's peace of mind.

The structural balance of the work is quite remarkable. Whereas the sections with expository material occupy 106 bars (approximately two fifths of the total length), the first development plus coda (71 bars) equals in dimension the second development plus modified recapitulation (76 bars), and these together constitute three fifths of the entire piece. The two developments are of equal length; the addition of the codalike section after the first development prevents the last two parts from being top-heavy and also provides a contrast that separates the two developments.

Webern's thematic process is strictly motivic. By repetition, sequence, and fragmentation into part motives, he obtains cohesion. No attempt is made to build larger units. The motives are short (1-2 bars) and are melodically and rhythmically well profiled. They appear with homophonic accompaniment or in imitative counterpoint—more often, however, in combinations. The texture becomes rather thick when two or three motives are played simultaneously. For contrast, Webern uses them also singly, soloistically, even without any accompaniment, especially in the loose transitional passages. Motive transformation is common; rhythmic changes often alter the character; part motives are used and assembled in new combinations. The sections are easily discernible, as the composer ends many of them with complete stops. In general, concise beginnings taper off thematically and in dynamics. Toward the end of the sections, the motives are strung together more loosely and the original impetus diminishes. Only twice are climaxes placed at the end of a section.

The harmonic vocabulary the composer used in this work is traditional late Romantic. The tertian principle of building triads and seventh chords is adhered to; the tonal functions are ever present. The only progressive element is the frequent, sometimes sudden, change of keys. The mediant relations, so dear to the Romanticists, abound. The scale degrees a third apart may be diatonic, or they may reach to the chromatic altered intervals. Webern uses comparatively few altered and "vagrant" chords (to use Schoenberg's terminology), however, and his harmonic idiom is much less chromatic than that of Wagner. The effective balance between harmonically static and dynamic sections proves the composer's feelings for necessary contrast. There are extended pedal points—as at the beginning and end—but also sections in lively harmonic rhythm. The bass line as a driving force for harmonic propulsion is well developed.

In the realm of sound and orchestration, *Im Sommerwind* shows many more facets pointing to the future than does the harmony. Webern asks for a large orchestra. The woodwinds consist of three flutes, two oboes and English horn, four clarinets (two in A, two in B flat), and bass clarinet, with only two bassoons. The lack of trombones and tubas in the brass group deviates from the norm. Only six horns and two trumpets are required. Never in the whole composition do we find the massive brass sound. Percussion instruments are also used in moderation: only timpani, triangle, and cymbal. The number of string players is large; multiple division makes this necessary. Two harps complete the orchestral body.

From a study of the orchestration, several factors become apparent. (1) The entire orchestra plays only rarely together. (2) Most instruments are used soloistically, or in groups of the same timbre (e.g., four horns, two clarinets). (3) Doubling is used sparingly, and then mostly between sound-related instruments. (4) Sound mixtures and color effects are not frequent.

The principle of delicate soloistic orchestration is especially prevalent in the more aphoristic, transitional passages. For instance, bars 34-44 of the score employ the following instruments: oboe solo (motive 3); clarinet solo (motivic fragment); four muted horns (motive 2); flute solo (motive 3); one pizzicato chord in cellos and basses; fourfold divided violins (motivic fragment); one cymbal stroke; four stopped horns (chromatic chord progressions); two notes in the flutes; arpeggio and *bispigliando* in two harps; and so forth. There is no accompaniment, and there are no sound blendings. It seems appropriate to compare this technique with the principle of *Klangfarbenmelodie* developed two decades later. Extreme ranges and special timbres of instruments are also introduced: mutes, natural harmonics and *sul ponticello* in the strings, muted and stopped brass. The sound of the orchestra is never conventional or dull, but always expressive, varied, and idiomatic for all instruments.

The range of dynamics is very wide. The composer's indications in the score are most specific, especially in the markings of soft sound. Webern reaches from simple *p* down to *ppp* and *kaum hörbar* ("barely audible"). At the end of the codalike section, and at the final end, the notation *bis zur gänzlichen Unhörbarkeit* ("until total inaudibility") reminds us of Webern's later characterization as the composer of the *pianissimo espressivo*. The expressive marks indeed are numerous, too: at some places *hervortretend* ("articulate"), more often *sehr zart und leise* ("very tender and soft"). The sensitivity to sound is one of the outstanding characteristics of this score.

The question has been posed as to whether it is appropriate that *Im Sommerwind,* an early work to which Webern assigned no opus number, should be performed and published. There are two reasons for answering in the affirmative. First, every extant product of a great composer has to be considered valuable. It is important for his artistic development, even if it is cast in the styles of previous musical epochs. The youthful works of Mozart, Beethoven, Bruckner have contributed much to our knowledge of their authors' growth. Later style characteristics of composers can be more easily recognized in the light of early compositions, which show the direction of development. Second, and especially in the case of Anton von Webern, some of these youthful compositions, among them *Im Sommerwind,* are fully developed in technical and emotional content and can provide a valuable artistic experience for the listener. The musical language may be different from that generally associated with this composer. But it will be remembered that even Arnold Schoenberg, the revered teacher of Webern, later in his life wrote the *Suite in G* for strings, and the *Theme and Variations* for band, both recognized as masterpieces.

LEONARD STEIN

Webern's *Dehmel Lieder* of 1906-8: Threshold of a New Expression

During the years of the composition of his five *Dehmel Lieder,* 1906-8, Anton von Webern, along with Alban Berg, was finishing his apprenticeship in composition under Arnold Schoenberg. As we know, this was a period of "crisis" in composition; the crucial changes of tonal concept initiated by Schoenberg in his "transitional" works of this time were to exert a potent influence on all of modern composition. But this influence was first felt most strongly by his two pupils, who shared directly in their master's discoveries.

In 1907 Schoenberg composed his second *String Quartet,* Opus 10, in F-sharp minor, the last two movements of which were written for soprano voice to texts of the German symbolist poet, Stefan George. The second of these movements, "Entrückung," is of special interest since it contains lengthy sections during which the consequences of tonal harmony are held in abeyance, so to speak, except for occasional triadic cadences reached by sudden and oblique routes, usually the product of highly chromatic progressions. (This is not to suggest that these cadences are not well prepared in terms of the composer's own vocabulary of "extended" tonality: see descriptions in Schoenberg's *Harmonielehre* and *Structural Functions of Harmony.*) The "compromise" with the tonal cadence is seen most clearly at the end of this movement—the conclusion of the entire quartet—when its principal figure, presented initially as a tonally ambiguous series of pitches, is resolved into F-sharp major, the tonic major key. Nontriadic chords, often consisting of superimposed fourths and major sevenths, and the permeating chromatic movement of parts add to the effect of tonal vagueness.

A similar procedure can be observed in Schoenberg's *George Lieder*, Opus 14, whose two songs are even more colored by nontriadic means than is Opus 10, particularly by fourth chords, but nevertheless end with a definite affirmation of the tonic triad. However, in the succeeding composition—fifteen songs from George's *Das Buch der hängenden Gärten*, Opus 15—Schoenberg emphatically breaks with the past and forswears any compromise with traditional tonality, although the means he employs, both harmonically and melodically, do not advance much beyond those of Opus 14.

In the works composed by Alban Berg during this period a similar evolution takes place. Berg's early *Lieder* (1905-8) show a gradual moving away from conventional triadic structure and tonal cadence, an increasing predilection for whole-tone and chromatic materials, and the construction of melodic lines with less conventional intervallic content. His *Sonata for Piano,* Opus 1 (1908), and the first three songs of Opus 2 still retain key signatures; but their harmonic structure, for the most part, defies tonal analysis—or, at least, leads to a multiplicity of analytical interpretations—except for the cadences. The last of the Opus 2 songs (text by Mombert) forgoes any reference to tonality by ending on a completely unresolved chord which, as in the Opus 15 songs of Schoenberg, is the resultant of the intervals featured in the course of the composition itself.

Webern participated in this movement of tonal crisis and transition with his recently published *Dehmel Lieder*, his *Passacaglia for Orchestra,* Opus 1 (1908), and his choral work *Entflieht auf leichten Kähnen,* Opus 2 (text by George), compositions that also exhibit the discovery of new means that are to open paths in the direction of his atonal songs, Opus 3 and Opus 4 (1909, texts also by George). The *Dehmel Lieder,* in particular, have considerable significance, not only as a link in the evolution of Webern's style, but also as one of the earliest examples of the composer's successful handling of the *Lied,* a genre to which he was to make some of the most original contributions of the twentieth century. By total count, Webern's output for voice consists of four published sets with piano and eight with diverse instrumental ensembles, as well as five choral works—numerically more than half of his listed *opera.* In addition there exist three earlier, and as yet unpublished, solo sets with piano, dating from 1899 to 1904, in the Moldenhauer Archive. At every stage of Webern's career vocal music assumed a role of great importance: the Opus 3 songs are his first atonal compositions; the third of his *Drei Volkstexte,* Opus 17 (with viola, clarinet, and bass clarinet), represents Webern's first attempt at twelve-tone composition; while the two cantatas, Opus 29 and Opus 31, along with the *Variations for Orchestra,* Opus 30, the last of his works, must be considered as the ultimate culmination of his style.

The compelling interest of Schoenberg, Berg, and Webern in the *Lied* may represent their desire not only to continue one of the great traditions of nineteenth-century music, assimilating the post-Wagnerian melos in the process, but also to take advantage of the flexibility of expression and construction allowed by a text. This reliance on a text to achieve new musical forms is acknowledged by Schoenberg in his essay "Composition with Twelve Tones."[1] Of course, with the German-Austrian composers this interest has always been dependent upon a poetic utterance typifying the *Stimmung* of the age, as illustrated by Schumann's affinity for the poetry of Heine, and Mahler's for *Des Knaben Wunderhorn.* Early in his career, Schoenberg was attracted to the neo-Romantic poetry of Richard Dehmel with its main expression of the mystical unity of man and nature, bridged by

[1] See *Style and Idea* (New York: Philosophical Library, 1950), p. 106.

human passions. Perhaps the most perfect representation of this poetry is to be found in one of Schoenberg's purely instrumental works, the string sextet *Verklärte Nacht,* which was composed in 1899 after Dehmel's text, *Zwei Menschen,* and was greatly admired by the poet himself.[2] In addition, Schoenberg made settings of five other Dehmel poems, which were published among the songs of Opus 2 and 3 (1899), and in Opus 6 (1905), as well as at least three others which have not been published.[3]

The hyperromantic settings of these poems were well known by Webern, who proceeded to make use of Dehmel's poetry for his own songs. Of the five poems he chose, four are derived from the collection *Weib und Welt;* the fifth, "Nächtliche Scheu," appears in the collection entitled *Aber die Liebe.* In general, these poems depict man's emotional accord with mystical aspects of nature. "Ideale Landschaft" is concerned with rejected love: "And always you looked away from me, / At the light, at the light— / And far off died the echo of my cry." "Nächtliche Scheu" presents an interesting simile comparing the timidity of the moonlight peering through the clouds and kissing the trembling waters, with the faint-hearted lover who kisses his sweetheart. "Am Ufer" is a reflection of the human soul as it aspires like a star from the depths of the sea to drink the sun's eternal light. In a similar manner, "Himmelfahrt" is concerned with the ecstatic ascension of the soul, blissfully immersed in the nightly expanse which reveals all mysteries beyond time. Finally, "Helle Nacht" is another scene from nature—"Softly the white moon kisses the boughs"—in which lovers are transported in their dreams.

It is significant that this hyperromantic world of ecstatic vision should have found its typical musical realization in the last remnants of a style—call it post-Romantic, or post-Wagnerian—in

[2] See Josef Rufer, *The Works of Arnold Schoenberg* (New York: Free Press of Glencoe, 1963), p. 24.

[3] *Ibid.,* pp. 98-99. These songs will soon appear in Vol. I of the *Collected Works* of Schoenberg (Mainz: B. Schott's Söhne).

these early songs of the later Viennese masters. The next phase, the atonal, leading to a style of more condensed expression ("Expressionism"), found its perfect wedding with the poetry of Stefan George (Schoenberg, Opera 10, 14, and 15; Webern, Opera 3 and 4)—poetry that emanates a more universal, more subtle, less naïvely passionate type of expression, in which the influence of the refined French Symbolist poets is so evident. Schoenberg himself recognized the importance of this new type of poetic expression to his music in an article he wrote for the *Blaue Reiter* —an issue that also contained one of his *George Lieder* of Opus 15: "With the George-Lieder I have succeeded for the first time in approaching an expressive and formal idea which has haunted me for years. . . . I am aware I have burst the bounds of bygone aesthetics." In like manner, Webern must have experienced this shifting of poetic and aesthetic emphasis. There is no doubt that the tendency of his musical style toward greater conciseness, gradual elimination of repetition and symmetry, sharpening of musical image, was to find its first most characteristic formulation through the poetry of Stefan George.

The *Dehmel Lieder* bring us, then, to the threshold of the first stage in the evolution of Webern's style. But even in these early songs we find characteristics that are typically Webern's own, distinct, in large part, from those of Schoenberg and Berg. For one thing, Webern is definitely more at home with the short, concise lyrical song, much less developed and dramatically inclined than many of the early songs of Schoenberg. The latter still contain numerous elements of repetition, sequence, motivic development, and other more traditional devices derived from thematic construction. Webern also appears to be much less interested than was Schoenberg in problems of a purely harmonic nature, such as the substitution of altered and ambiguous chords for traditional chords and their usual root progressions. However, the indirect and often abrupt approaches to tonal cadences are similar to those employed in Schoenberg's "transitional" works, mentioned previously. Chromatic part leading, which plays such a large role in connecting chords, particularly of nontriadic varieties, in the songs of Schoenberg, assumes lesser importance in the *Dehmel Lieder*. Similarly, the complexity and richness of chordal texture that is so typical of some of the early songs of Berg, in Opus 2 especially, is generally of secondary interest in these songs of Webern. Certain novel chordal and intervallic combinations do appear consistently in the latter, but in no manner approaching the highly chromatic combinations of Schoenberg, nor his characteristic usages of chords built up of fourths or major sevenths, for example. Webern often prefers chord constructions derived from the whole-tone scale, with their major thirds and augmented triads (see Example 1, "Nächtliche Scheu," beginning). Where

Example 1. Webern, Nächtliche Scheu

cross-related major sevenths or minor ninths occur, as in "Am Ufer," they are treated as constructive sonorities in their own right. Truly complex sonorities are encountered but infrequently; much more characteristic are reinforcements of chordal elements by added thirds, sixths, or octaves, as in Example 2. Through such means a certain transparency of sound usually results.

It is in the realm of contrapuntal treatment, of course, that these songs of Webern bear the closest resemblance to those of Schoenberg. Imitation between voice and accompaniment is the

Example 2. Webern, Himmelfahrt (piano only)

principal technical feature in at least four of the songs, while all of them contain nearly continuous movement with two or three real independent parts. The last song of the set, "Helle Nacht," is a veritable tour de force of writing in double counterpoint between voice and piano.

In vocal writing, again, the style of Webern diverges somewhat from that of his master. To a great extent, the vocal writing of Schoenberg's preatonal period is post-Wagnerian, with its intensely expressive, large-spanned melodies, featuring many leaps, frequent climaxes, and chromatic convolutions growing out of the underlying harmonic web. Webern's style is of a simpler sort: the vocal line often compensates for large leaps by stepwise motion; the vocal range is more confined (unlike Webern's own later writing for voice!). The most Schoenberg-like song, "Himmelfahrt," with its leaps and frequent sequences producing one climax upon another, is probably the least successful of the entire set.

In the attempt to establish closer organic relationships by development from a single motive, introduced either by the voice or by the accompaniment, we find an early intimation of Webern's later style, a step toward greater unity and concisiveness. Traditional accompaniment figures in regular pattern—usually triplets or afterbeating syncopated chords—are gradually replaced by a more perfectly realized contrapuntal way of writing in the piano part, so that in the last song, "Helle Nacht," every note more nearly assumes its significant relationship with the whole.

The construction of all the songs, with the exception of the last, falls within the flexible boundaries of A-B-A or ternary form. However, the recapitulations are always well disguised and usually lead to different continuations before the final cadence. In "Helle Nacht," on the other hand, each of its three sections consists of varied repetitions with voice and accompaniment appearing in invertible counterpoint. The two main melodic strands are presented in the familiar Webern dichotomy of three-against-two. Each section of this song is prefaced by a short phrase or motive built upon a type of progression and certain timbres that clearly forecast similar means in the Opus 3 songs (see Example 3). Actually, each stanza leads directly to this phrase, creating a parallel construction with the short line of text at the end of each stanza: "*Geliebte du*" (probably the source of this phrase) at the end of the first stanza; "*Wir träumen, wir träumen*" at the end of the second; and "*O hin, O Traum*" at the very end. The literal repetition of this phrase, however, occurs only in the piano part, the vocal part being constantly varied, as is true throughout most of these songs. The ending of the third stanza presents only the rising tritone of the phrase in the voice.

Example 3. Webern, Helle Nacht

And, most significant of all—reminding one of the last of the Mombert songs of Berg—"Helle Nacht" ends on an unresolved chord, which comes from the ending chord of the opening phrase: an augmented triad superimposed on a tritone. Webern retains the key signature of D minor for this song, and to a certain extent we might assume that the final chord represents the leading tone of that key, C sharp. But, unlike all the other songs, the lack of consequences of traditional harmony and of triadic emphasis throughout this song abnegates once and for all any definite affinity or necessity for a tonal center. Thus we are led, in this last Dehmel song, to the threshold of the "true" Webern style, and to his mature manner of expression and use of musical means.

WALLACE McKENZIE

Webern's Technique of Choral Composition

Of Webern's thirty-one published compositions with opus numbers, five are for chorus. These five choral works cover the span of Webern's creative life from 1908 to 1943, although not every phase of his compositional development is represented. The earliest work for chorus, *Entflieht auf leichten Kähnen,* Opus 2 (1908), for a cappella mixed chorus, is one of two early works that are tonal in the traditional sense. The next choral work does not come until after the long, free atonal period, when, in 1926, the *Two Songs,* Opus 19, for mixed chorus accompanied by an instrumental ensemble, appears. This composition represents the formative stage of Webern's use of the twelve-tone technique as seen in Opera 17-20.

The remaining three choral works, *Das Augenlicht,* Opus 26 (1935), and the two cantatas, Opus 29 (1939) and Opus 31 (1943), were all composed when Webern's style and technique were fully developed. It is in these works, all three of which use the poetry of Hildegard Jone, that a choral technique that is unique in its varieties of imitation, in its harmonic structure, and in its adaptation of pre-existing choral forms and techniques may be seen. And it is the treatment of the chorus in these three works with which this study is primarily concerned.

Before investigating Webern's choral technique it may be worthwhile to consider, at least briefly, the vocal style found in the many songs composed from 1908 to 1925. This style involves characteristics that to some extent may also be found in the vocal music of Arnold Schoenberg, particularly, for example, in *Herzgewächse*, Opus 20 (1911). Beginning with the second song of Opus 8 (1910), the vocal lines in the songs of Webern contain many skips of a major seventh, minor ninth, and larger intervals in quickly moving notes, and fast passages that span the extended range of the voice. (See, for example, in Opus 18, No. 2, "Erlösung," measure 10, where the vocal line covers a span of two octaves and a perfect fifth—*d'''* down to *g*—within the time of one measure.) Also to be mentioned are the occasional instances of word painting. (See, for example, in each of the *Five Sacred Songs*, Opus 15, the heavenlike arches that occur with the various forms of the word *"Himmel."*) There are few purely dramatic devices in the vocal lines, although one may find isolated, quasi-recitative sections (e.g., Opus 12, No. 4, "Gleich und Gleich," measures 13-14, marked *"frei"*), and other places where dramatic relief is given certain words (e.g., Opus 13, No. 3, "In der Fremde," measures 17-18, the setting of *"der Mond"*). The basic nature of the lines in the songs is lyrical, and this nature is perhaps best exemplified by a particular melodic configuration that occurs in varied forms, again and again, not only in the songs and choral works, but in all of Webern's music from the early *Piano Quintet* (1906) through the *Second Cantata*. Indeed, this melodic shape, which may be described as consisting basically of two descending intervals, a small plus a large, followed by upward movement, is so much an identifying part of Webern's melos that it may well be called a "signature phrase" (Example 1).

Example 1. Webern: (a) Five Songs, Op. 3, No. 3, meas. 13-14;
(b) Four Songs, Op. 13, No. 4, meas. 6-7

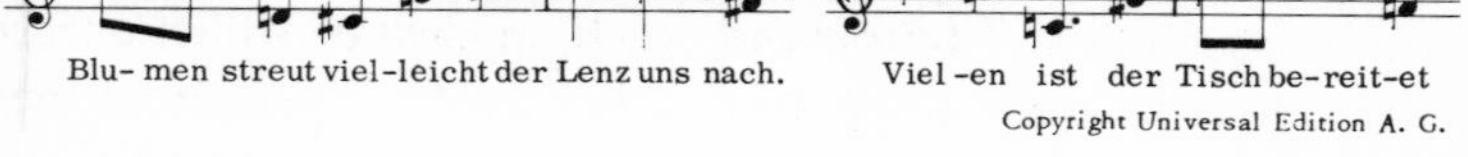
(a)
ppp
3
Blu- men streut viel-leicht der Lenz uns nach.
(b) pp
Viel -en ist der Tisch be-reit-et

That Webern valued highly pre-existing forms, schemes, and devices is clearly indicated by his continuous use of them throughout his music, and, of these, his concern with varieties of imitation is perhaps the most strongly evident. The a cappella chorus, Opus 2, is canonic throughout. There are two canons within a ternary form: the first one is a two-part canon in which each part is doubled at the third, and the second one is in four parts. The imitation is real and direct: there is no imitation by contrary motion or retrograde.

Perhaps the most interesting thing about Opus 2 is the way in which the doubling lines function. At the beginning, the alto doubles the soprano a third below, and the tenor doubles the answering bass a sixth above. However, very soon the tenor and bass lines exchange functions so that, in measure 3, the tenor is answering the soprano, and the bass is doubling the tenor a third below. Changes such as this occur frequently. Also, there are several places (e.g., measures 3, 8, 20) where the doubling parts deviate from strict doubling—always in strict imitation of each other. The result is that, while the first and third sections are essentially two-part canons doubled at the third, much of the time the texture is that of a four-part, double canon.

In contrast to Opus 2, the two Goethe *Songs*, Opus 19—the second choral work that Webern wrote—contain no canons and no exact imitation. There are places in both songs where the voices enter one after the other in a manner suggesting imitation (see No. 1, measures 17 ff., and No. 2, measures 15 ff.), but they are quite free. Only occasional similarities of rhythm and contour are present. As indicated above, this is some of Webern's early twelve-tone music, and it is structurally quite unlike any of the other choral works. In the first song, for example, the soprano line is the principal one, and it is accompanied, or answered antiphonally, by the other three voices. The accompanying parts form short phrases of four chords each, in each of which phrases the twelve-tone series is deployed rather freely. Throughout these two songs the voices are doubled by instruments, but the doubling is always in a different rhythm from that of the voices and contains many repeated notes.

Webern's next choral work, *Das Augenlicht* (1935), Opus 26, is a single-movement piece in motet style; that is, imitative polyphonic sections are interspersed with chordal sections throughout the piece. In the first choral phase of the motet, measures 8-13, in which only the soprano and tenor voices participate, one may find the first example of the type of canonic structure with which Webern was concerned in his last three choral works (Example 2). It may be noticed that the rhythm of the

Example 2. Webern, Das Augenlicht, Op. 26, meas. 8-13, vocal lines

answering voice (tenor) imitates the rhythm of the leading voice (soprano) exactly and directly with the same text. The melodic shape of the tenor line at the beginning gives the impression of being a varied inversion of the soprano line, but the pitches of the tenor part form an exact retrograde of those of the soprano. This structure becomes possible through the use of two forms (in this case, the retrograde inversion and the inversion) of the twelve-tone series.

Although the shapes of the two lines are not imitated exactly, either in contrary motion or in retrograde, there are several imitative fragments. Notice, for example, fragments *a* and *b*, which are exactly imitative in retrograde, and which are related to each other by direct imitation of a single interval—involving the same notes in each case. Besides this, at the mid-point of the phrase, both lines converge on the same pitch (marked *X* in Example 2). Thus, with the relatively simple deployment of one form of the series and its retrograde, a phrase is formed which contains a multiplicity of interrelationships.

The same procedure is followed in the second phrase (measures 14-19) and in the phrase beginning in measure 104 with somewhat different interrelationships. With the exception of two short sections near the end (measures 85-87 and 96-99), in which the imitation of melodic contour is direct and exact, the imitative sections all employ direct imitation of the rhythmic and inexact melodic imitation.

The homophonic sections of *Das Augenlicht* are almost entirely unaccompanied, the single exception being the climax phrase, "*O Meer des Blickes mit der Tränenbrandung*" (measures 64-69).[1] The chords of the homophonic sections, with very few exceptions, contain one or two chromatic intervals, usually major sevenths or minor ninths. This, of course, is true of all of Webern's harmonic structures after Opus 2.

Perhaps the most notable characteristic of the homophonic sections of this work is the frequent use of the first five notes of the original form of the series in the soprano line. Phrases that contain this contour may be found beginning in measures 20, 30 (see Example 3), 64, and 87. The exact shape is also found at the

Example 3. Webern, Das Augenlicht, Op. 26, meas. 30-32

[1] Webern indicated, in a letter to Hildegard Jone, October 15, 1935, that this was the first section of Opus 26 that he composed (Anton Webern, *Briefe an Hildegard Jone und Josef Humplik,* ed. Josef Polnauer [Vienna: Universal Edition, 1959], p. 32).

beginning of the single bass line in measures 77-79. Frequent exact recurrences of specific melodic shapes of this length, and with this small range, are exceptionally rare in the music of Webern.

The *First Cantata,* Opus 29, is a three-movement work in which the first and third movements are choral.[2] The nature of the first movement is that of a dramatic recitative. It is, in fact, quite pictorial in the sense of a pastoral scene. After a twelve-measure introductory, instrumental section—in which soft, sustained chordal phrases are interspersed with loud, polyphonic sections, and which ends with a low sforzando note on muted trombone, followed by a fortissimo stroke on the timpani along with a cymbal crash—the mixed chorus enters, a cappella, at measure 14, with the words *"Zündender Lichtblitz"* (Example 4). The effect is graphically that of the approach and arrival of a storm. But, of course, this is not just an ordinary electrical storm. Rather, it is the "Kindling lightning of Being, which strikes from the storm cloud of the word" (measures 14-22). Webern's intense concern and love for the elements and products of nature, such as colors and flowers, as well as his strong, generally traditional, religious faith, are continually in evidence in his vocal and choral works. In the two cantatas, through the poetry of Jone, these two basic concerns are fused.

All of the choral phrases of the first movement are chordal. They are almost entirely homorhythmic, although they are not, in a strict sense, homophonic. The first choral phrase (Example 4) contains several constructive ideas that Webern had not used before in his choral music. In the first two measures and the last three measures, the two basic melodic contours, each doubled at the interval of a major ninth, occur simultaneously. In the central part of the phrase the voices shift out of phase with each other, and the relationships of the melodic contours change. The tenor and bass lines imitate in contrary motion the exact contour of the alto and soprano lines, respectively, in measures 16-17; then the

[2] The second movement is a soprano solo with orchestra.

Example 4. Webern, First Cantata, Op. 29, No. 1, meas. 14-22

S.
A.
T.
B.
Zün-den-der Licht-blitz des Le - bens schlug
ein aus der Wol - ke des Wort-es
Copyright Universal Edition A. G.

The numerals 1. 2. 1., 3. 4. 3., etc., refer to chordal structures explained later in the present discussion.

imitation is reversed. Here (measures 18-19) the greatest degree of identity among the four lines is attained because the shapes and interval content of all four lines are identical, although the bass and alto lines move in opposite direction to the others. Also, the first and last notes of two parts are the same as the last and first notes of the other two in these measures. The result is that each line is related to the other by direct imitation, imitation in contrary motion, and retrograde.

What is perhaps of equal importance in this movement, with this sort of complex canon where the time intervals vary from zero to one-quarter-note value, is the harmonic structure.[3] For, in the choral sections, there occur only six different four-note chords as defined by pitch content. Through the crossing of voices, the interval organization changes from time to time; but each vertical complex of the chorus has a pitch content of one of only six basic chords. Clearly, if two or more lines, using a twelve-tone series in one of its four forms, continue consistently at the same interval from each other, as they do here, then the number of different vertical complexes possible is limited. But the normal minimum number in this situation (as may be seen in the *Second Cantata,* Opus 31, No. 3) is twelve, the number of notes in a twelve-tone series. The reason that the number here is six lies in the symmetrical structure of the series.[4] Significantly, the chords here always occur in symmetrical groups, such as 1-2-1, 3-4-3, and so forth (see Example 4).

The other choral movement of Opus 29, No. 3, was called by Webern a four-voice fugue. He also used the terms "scherzo" and "variations" as he described it to Jone; "but," he said, it is "still a fugue."[5] The choral sections of this movement are mostly polyphonic and involve generally the same type of imitative relationships as those in Opus 26.

In all of Opus 29 Webern uses the twelve-tone series in such a way that the last two notes of one form become the first two notes of another. In the two polyphonic phrases of the third movement the deployment of the series forms creates another kind of symmetry. During the first choral phrase, for example, each of the

[3] For a recent study of the harmony of this movement, see George Rochberg's "Webern's Search for Harmonic Identity," *Journal of Music Theory,* Spring, 1962, pp. 109-24.

[4] The last six notes of the series of Opus 29 form a transposed retrograde inversion of the first six, so that the inversion and retrograde forms of the series are identical in structure.

[5] Webern, *Briefe,* Letter of December 2, 1939, p. 41.

two basic lines derives from three statements of the series in the order retrograde–original–retrograde, and the transpositions of the series are so arranged that in the third statement each voice begins with the same note as that with which the other began in the first statement.[6] Or, to put it another way, that which led at the beginning follows at the end. A similar situation is found in the second choral phrase (measures 39-53), although it is more extended.

Webern's last choral work, the *Second Cantata,* Opus 31, is also his last completed composition. Considered superficially, it is unique among Webern's works in several respects. It is the longest opus in time of performance, lasting about ten and one-half minutes.[7] Also, it is the only work in which Webern wrote specifically for bass solo (Nos. 1 and 2), and the only time he wrote for women's chorus (No. 3). Finally, the last movement (No. 6) is repeated exactly, twice, without any variation other than the text.

Webern has explained the basic structures of the six movements of the *Second Cantata* in letters to Hildegard Jone and Willi Reich. In these explanations one may frequently see his concern for multifarious explanations and descriptions of the movements, which also seem to reflect the concern in his music for manifold and formal constructive relationships. The first two movements are for bass solo and orchestra: a recitative and aria.[8]

[6] The symmetry is more clearly seen as follows:

R-4, answered by R-10
O-8, answered by O-2
R-10, answered by R-4.

[7] This is the time required for the performance in "Anton Webern: The Complete Music," Columbia Records No. K4L-232, directed by Robert Craft. Webern, in a letter to Willi Reich, February 23, 1944, estimated the length of Opus 31 to be a half hour (quoted in Anton Webern, *Der Weg zur neuen Musik,* ed. Willi Reich [Vienna: Universal Edition, 1960], p. 73).

[8] Webern, *Briefe,* Letter to Jone, September 4, 1942, p. 50. In a letter to Willi Reich, August 6, 1943 (*Der Weg zur neuen Musik,* p. 70), Webern explains that the bass aria (No. 2), while it is basically a free, infinite, double canon in contrary motion with variation, diminution, and so forth, "some-

The third movement is for women's chorus, soprano solo, and orchestra. Movement No. 4, for soprano solo, is also an introduction or recitative.[9] It introduces the fifth movement, for soprano solo, mixed chorus, solo violin obbligato, and orchestra. The sixth and final movement, for chorus and orchestra, Webern called a "chorale,"[10] although he said it should not be thought of in the sense of a Bach chorale. After the completion of Opus 31, Webern wrote Jone another description of the total work which will be discussed after an examination of the choral sections of the cantata.

The women's chorus (No. 3), in three parts—soprano I, soprano II, and alto—is polyphonic throughout. For some reason, perhaps partially because of the monochromatic quality of women's voices alone, Webern chose not to write any chordal sections in this movement. The movement begins with a four-part canon in the following order: soprano II, instruments (beginning with the French horn), alto, and soprano I.

The line carried by the orchestra is changed from one instrument to another in the *Klangfarbenmelodie* manner in such a way that the changes of timbre do not always correspond with the phrases of the vocal lines. The vocal lines are doubled by instruments in the same manner, and certain fragments, such as the two notes with the first word of the text, *"Schöpfen,"* are doubled by more than one instrument. The vocal lines are always doubled at the same pitch, never at a different octave. This is true of every case in the choral works of Webern where the choral parts are doubled by instruments (Opus 19; Opus 29, No. 3; Opus 31, Nos. 3 and 6), and, except for the *Two Songs,* Opus 19, the instrumen-

---

what as Bach proceeds with his theme in the Art of Fugue," it is formally a three-part aria with a periodic theme of about thirty-two measures and has the character of a hymn.

[9] Webern, *Der Weg zur neuen Musik,* Letter to Willi Reich, August 23, 1941, p. 69; *Briefe,* Letter to Jone, August 13, 1941, pp. 47-48.

[10] Webern, *Briefe,* Letter to Jone, September 4, 1942, p. 50.

tal parts have basically the same rhythm as the voices. The instrumental doubling of the vocal parts seems to have two purposes, one practical and one musical. The obvious practical purpose is that of assisting the singers with their pitches, and the musical purpose, which is perhaps more important, is that of underlining the sounds with varying qualities of articulation and timbre. In this chorus certain notes of the instrumental canonic line are also doubled (see, for example, measure 4).

The series structure of the third movement of Opus 31 is similar in principle to that of the third movement of Opus 29. In the first point of imitation all four parts derive from the same forms of the series. These forms occur in the symmetrical order retrograde–inversion–retrograde. In fact, each of the four sections of the movement involves three series forms, each time in a different order, as follows: (1) R–I–R, (2) O–RI–O, (3) RI–O–RI, and (4) I–R–I. Thus, another symmetry presents itself, wherein the orders of the third section (RI–O–RI) and fourth section (I–R–I) are inversions of the orders of the second section (O–RI–O) and first section (R–I–R). At the same time the forms of the second and fourth sections are retrogrades of the forms of the first and third sections, respectively.[11]

Webern's treatment of the twelve-tone series in such a way that a limited number of vertical complexes are employed in the choral parts of a movement was discussed above in connection with Opus 29, No. 1. This treatment may be seen again in the fifth movement of the *Second Cantata*, which, like the third movement of Opus 29, is also homorhythmic. Here, through octave displacements of some notes of the series, two distinct melodic lines are formed, one carried by the soprano (with the alto

[11] Again, these relationships are more clearly seen as follows:

1. R—I—R
2. O—RI—O
3. RI—O—RI
4. I—R—I.

doubling at the interval of a minor seventh), and the other by the tenor (with the bass doubling at the interval of a major seventh); both lines derive from the simultaneous deployment of the same form of the series (Example 5). Webern said about this

Example 5. Webern, Second Cantata, Op. 31, No. 5: (a) meas. 1-3; (b) meas. 46-47

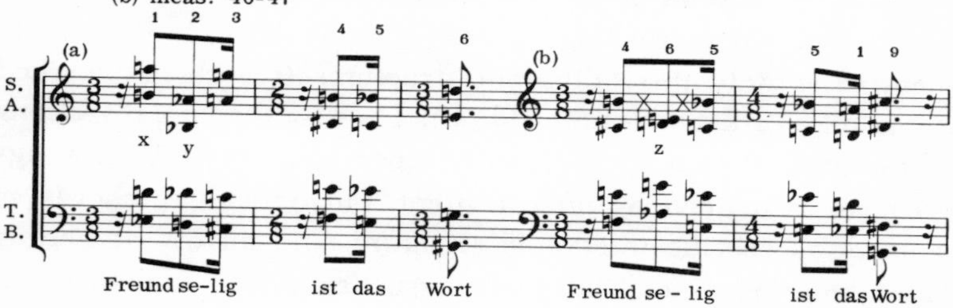

chorus, "I believe I might say that I succeed in an *entirely new* style of representation: for on a *purely polyphonic* basis, I arrive at the exact opposite kind of representation."[12]

The "opposite kind of representation" mentioned here must have to do with the harmonic structure. In the choral sections of this movement there are only twelve different vertical aggregates (i.e., chords defined by pitch content), all of the same basic intervallic structure; but the order of occurrence of the aggregates differs with every transposition and every change of series form. The result is a limited number of different vertical complexes, recurring in ever changing order. To illustrate, if the vertical aggregates, or chords, are numbered 1-12, the sequence of occurrence in the chordal sections of Opus 31, No. 5, begins as follows: 1-2-3-4-5-6, 7-3-4-5-8, 3-4-8-5-6-9-10-11, and so forth (Example 5). To realize the variety of sequences more vividly, one may consider the immediate environment of any particular chord as it recurs. Chord No. 5, for example, occurs in this movement as the central chord in the following groups of three: 4-5-6, 4-5-8, 8-5-6,

[12] Webern, *Briefe*, Letter to Jone, June 3, 1942, p. 49.

4-5-1, 6-5-1, and 2-5-4. Of course, although it may almost seem so, the orders of occurrence are not random, and the number of possible successions is not infinite.[13]

Because each of the vertical aggregates contains the same general intervallic orientation as the others, the only possibilities for altering the specific intervallic structure of a chord lie in the crossing of voices. Of these possibilities, Webern, in this movement, uses only three different structures (see chords marked *x*, *y*, and *z* of Examples 5a and 5b). Thus, in the choral sections of the fifth movement of Opus 31, there are twelve vertical aggregates as defined by pitch content, but only three chords as defined by specific intervallic structure, and all of the chords have the same general intervallic structure owing to their being formed by the simultaneous deployment of transpositions of the same form of the series.

In the final movement of Opus 31, the "Chorale," one may see a crystallization of several facets of Webern's choral technique. The type of quasi-canonic imitation seen in Opus 26, in Opus 29, No. 3, and in the third movement of this work is the basis for this final movement. The text consists of three short verses, for each of which the music repeats exactly. The voices are doubled by the instruments, and there is no other instrumental figuration. The "Chorale" is simply a four-part, twelve-tone canon in which the rhythm is imitated exactly, the pitches are imitated in two different sequences (a double canon), and the shapes, or contours, of the lines are only very freely imitated. However, the relationships are a little more complex than this indicates for, although only two different forms of the series are present at any time, the pitches of the bass and alto parts form a retrograde of those of the soprano and tenor parts, respectively. The result is that the leading voice (tenor) is imitated—in pitch

[13] Any particular chord may occur as the central chord in 110 (i.e., 11 x 10) different three-chord groups, and the number of possible different successions of the twelve chords is 12 factorial (479,001,600).

successions, not contour—in retrograde by the alto, directly by the soprano (at a major third), and in inversion by the bass (beginning on the same note).

The voices are doubled by instruments throughout the movement, and the timbres change much in the same way that they do in others of Webern's choral sections. However, here the timbre changes are more limited, for each choral part is doubled only by certain instruments in alternation with each other. The soprano is doubled by the oboe and first violin; the alto by the clarinet, trumpet, and second violin; the tenor by the saxophone, French horn, and viola; and the bass by the bass clarinet, trombone, and cello.

One of the more interesting aspects of the melodic lines is the rhythm. There is actually no meter, although frequently changing measure lengths, with single numbers given to indicate the number of pulses in each, are employed independently in the separate lines. Stresses coincide with the syllabic stresses of the text—a sort of *vers mesuré*—and they are so ordered that, even while all four parts are singing, each stress is heard through the texture.

This movement is indeed a crystallization of many facets of Webern's technique. But it is even more: it is something of an abstraction of his technique, for many of the variables normally expected in Webern's music are more nearly constant here. There are no changes of tempo, there are fewer dynamic changes—only a single crescendo and decrescendo near the mid-point—and all the instruments play without mutes, which, in the cases of the trumpet and trombone, is indeed rare.

The textual material for the *Second Cantata,* as for all the previous choral and vocal works since Opus 23 (1934), is supplied by Hildegard Jone. The sentiment of the poetry in Opus 31 is decidedly Christian, particularly in the third, fifth, and final movements. That Webern was concerned with the content of these expressions is adequately substantiated in his discussions of the poems in the letters to Jone. In a letter of January 28, 1944, he suggests that the six movements of Opus 31, as finally arranged, produce a *Missa brevis.*[14] Thus Webern perceives another formal description of the *Second Cantata,* Opus 31.

In conclusion, some general observations about texture in Webern's choral music may be appropriate. He never wrote for a divided chorus, or for more than four parts, except for the last four measures of Opus 2, where the bass part divides. He never wrote for male chorus, and there is only one example of a women's chorus (Opus 31, No. 3). The choral music is almost entirely in four parts: even in the three-part women's chorus the polyphonic texture is that of four melodic lines because of the concurrent sounding of a single instrumental line. This points to another significant consideration, namely, that in almost all of the choral music, whether basically contrapuntal or chordal, there is a certain ambiguity of texture owing to the possibility of dual and sometimes multiple interpretations. For example, in the first choral work, Opus 2, the two-part canon, in which each part is doubled at the third, tends to give the impression of a four-part double canon because of occasional deviations in the doubling voices. The homorhythmic sections of the two cantatas (Opus 29, No. 1; and Opus 31, No. 5) may be interpreted as progressions of four-part chords and at the same time as two-part counterpoint, with each part doubled at a certain interval; or, again, as a four-part double canon with interval of entry zero.

It seems that there actually exists in all of Webern's music the

[14] Webern, *Briefe,* pp. 54-55. In the letter Webern presents the parts in an outline as follows:

1. "Schweigt auch die Welt . . ." (bass solo)	Kyrie
2. "Sehr tief verhalten . . ." (bass solo)	Gloria
3. "Schöpfen aus Brunnen des Himmels . . ." (women's chorus with soprano solo)	Credo
4. "Leichteste Bürden der Bäume . . ." (soprano solo)	Benedictus
5. "Freundselig ist das Wort . . ." (soprano solo and chorus)	Sanctus
6. "Gelockert aus dem Schosse . . ." (chorus)	Agnus Dei

possibility, even the necessity, of multiple interpretations and explanations at all levels of analysis. As has been pointed out above, Webern, himself, frequently presented several interpretations and explanations for the same piece in his letters to Jone and Reich, and the existence of multifarious relationships at all levels is particularly significant in Webern's technique of choral composition.

WILLIAM AUSTIN

Webern and the Tradition of the Symphony

What has Webern to do with the tradition of the symphony? We may safely assume that something similar is intended when anyone speaks of the tradition of the symphony from Haydn down to Brahms, Bruckner, Dvořák, and Tchaikovsky. This tradition undoubtedly continues further, into our own time. But our views of it naturally differ widely.

If we see it embodied chiefly in a series of works by such a composer as Sibelius or Shostakovich, Vaughan Williams, Honegger, Walter Piston, William Schuman, then the one extraordinary symphony by Anton Webern hardly fits. In the tradition seen from those various points of view, Webern has found only a small and marginal place, if any at all. Indeed, he seems to stand in opposition to the tradition, attracting young listeners and composers and scholars toward chamber music and a strange new lyricism, even farther away from the public drama of the symphony.

If, on the other hand, we think of a tradition broader than that of the symphony itself—a line connecting Beethoven with Liszt and Wagner, then Mahler and Debussy, then Schoenberg and Stravinsky, Bartók, Berg, Milhaud, Hindemith—listeners and scholars interested in Webern are actively engaged in fitting him in, finding his proper place. We are ready, if need be, to relegate the symphony to a somewhat lower rank in our scheme of values than it holds on the market of concert tickets and phonograph records. We may even be ready to exalt Webern to a position alongside Bach, Josquin des Prez, Guillaume de Machaut, in an imaginary line connecting the summits of the various formal and stylistic traditions of Western music.

Webern's work has been called "the most representative musical product of our times,"[1] "the only threshold" to the music of the future,[2] and "the central point from which . . . most of the significant composition of the last decade or so can be measured."[3] In these sympathetic views, just as much as in the views of the devotees of Sibelius or Shostakovich, any connection between Webern and the tradition handed down from Haydn to the end of the nineteenth century seems tenuous and perhaps negligible.

The view of Webern himself, as far as it can be known up to now, was different from any of these views current today. His view is not yet widely known, for he expressed it privately, and it is only within the last few years that notes from his lectures and excerpts from his letters have been published. But here we find him declaring to a group of friends that Beethoven achieved a perfection and purity of form which is still fundamental for Mahler, Schoenberg, Berg, and himself.[4]

> Of course [he says] a symphony of Mahler looks different in comparison with one of Beethoven, but in essence, it is the same. . . . Even the modern symphony rests simply on these forms, and no one racks his brain to find something new. It is rather the tendency of the last few years to adhere to these forms quite strictly. . . . The

[1] Edward A. Lippman, review in *Musical Quarterly*, XL (1958), 418.

[2] Pierre Boulez, "Hommage à Webern," *Domaine musical*, I (1954), 123-25; reprinted in *Die Reihe* (German, 1955; English, 1958). Boulez reiterates his formula in the excellent article, "Webern," in the *Encyclopédie Fasquelle*, III (1961), 907-12.

[3] Leonard Stein, program notes for the post-Webern concert in the First Webern Festival, Seattle, 1962.

[4] Anton Webern, *Der Weg zur neuen Musik*, ed. Willi Reich (Vienna: Universal Edition, 1960), p. 28.

> style that Schoenberg and his school seek is a new penetration of the musical material in the horizontal and vertical, a polyphony that up to now has found its peaks with the Netherlanders and Bach, and then again with the classics. Always the urge to derive as much as possible from the main idea. It must be said so, for we are writing the very forms of the classicists; they are not at all finished with. Everything that they found by way of elaborate forms, is found also in New Music. It is not a matter of reconquest or reawakening of the Netherlanders, but of a new filling of their forms by way of the classics, a combination of both these things. It is naturally not a purely polyphonic thinking; it is both together. Thus we want to insist: we have not departed from the forms of the classics.[5]

Writing to his pupil, Willi Reich, Webern compares his *Variations for Orchestra*, Opus 30, with Beethoven's *Prometheus Overture* and Brahms's *Tragic Overture*.[6] He points out that on first glance his score looks utterly different from a score of Richard Strauss, different from Beethoven, different even from Bach.

> Is it something like an orchestrated Josquin? The answer must be an energetic "NO!" What then? Something unique. Now I should say decisively: Mine is music that rests just as much upon the laws established by musical expression *after* the Netherlanders, that by no means denies the development that came then, but rather tries to carry it further. . . .[7]

Writing to his friend Hildegard Jone, painter and poet, Webern speaks of having just finished his symphony; he identifies his striving for clarity with that shown in Beethoven's sketches for the *Eroica Symphony;* he insists that he and Schoenberg and Berg are striving always to achieve the same *sense* as the masters of the recent past, only with their own means.[8] In a later letter Webern tells Frau Jone about the work that was to become *Can-*

[5] *Ibid.*, pp. 35, 37.

[6] Letters published by Willi Reich as supplement to *ibid.*, p. 67.

[7] *Ibid.*, p. 67.

[8] Anton Webern, *Briefe an Hildegard Jone und Josef Humplik* (Vienna: Universal Edition, 1959), p. 10.

tata I, Opus 29; he calls it "a big symphonic cycle . . . a sort of symphony with vocal parts."[9]

Such statements may well inspire us to reconsider the music in the context of Webern's stylistic development through the course of his life. It was surely a marvelous development, from the student works—like *Im Sommerwind*, which came to life at last in 1962, in all the glorious sound of the Straussian orchestra—through the great *Passacaglia*, Opus 1, which is so indebted to the finale of Brahms's *Fourth Symphony*,[10] through the thrilling *Six Pieces for Large Orchestra*, Opus 6, and the fully mature *Five Pieces for Small Orchestra*, Opus 10, to the *Symphony*, Opus 21, and the last works. At the present stage of our understanding of Webern, however, it seems to me wise to neglect chronology and, in the light of the statements quoted above, to consider parts of three orchestra works, chosen to bring out certain characteristic traits of instrumentation, melody, and form.

For instrumentation, consider Webern's orchestral arrangement of Bach's six-voice ricercar. On first hearing, this instrumentation is shocking. Nothing reminds us of an organ. Nothing resembles the big sound of Strauss, or of Berg's *Lulu*, or of an Ormandy transcription of Bach. Yet there is also nothing like the instrumentation of Bach himself in his cantatas and concertos. Within every phase of melody Webern varies the color. Each motive is played by a different instrument, contrasting sometimes subtly and sometimes obviously with its immediate predecessor. Webern's purpose, he explained to the conductor Scherchen, was "to reveal the motivic coherence," and "to indicate the way I feel the character of the piece."[11]

Until we get used to this procedure, motives hardly cohere at all but rather stick out from the lines they belong to, whether

[9] *Ibid.*, p. 38.

[10] Walter Kolneder, *Anton Webern: Einführung in Werk und Stil* (Rodenkirchen am Rhein: P. J. Tonger, 1961), pp. 19-21, elaborates this comparison.

[11] Letter to Hermann Scherchen in *Die Reihe*, II (1955), 25-26.

these are subject or counterpoint. The "character" that Webern feels is astonishingly Romantic, poignant, fluctuating. The muted brass—never used by Bach—may even strike us as perverse. But on repeated hearings we must admit that this instrumentation makes every note clear and every chord significant. Nothing is merely completing a chord. Nothing is overwhelmed in the rich counterpoint. Nothing is emphasized at the expense of the counterpoint. The muted brasses are especially useful for cutting through a dense sound. They can serve in equality with woodwinds and strings, providing a wide range of colors without difference of weight.

The continually shifting colors, it turns out, serve the unity of the whole piece better than this could be served by contrasts more widely spaced. So we come to accept the sacrifice of obvious continuity within the subject, and we are well repaid. In the long run, studying the score as we listen, we may recover this continuity without giving up any of the new gains. Webern's arrangement can teach us to play or hear the ricercar on a keyboard instrument better than we did before. It is a marvel of musicianship and of living tradition.

To associate Webern's characteristic sounds and fluctuation of sounds with Bach's melody and counterpoint is a good preparation for listening to Webern's own *Klangfarbenmelodie.* Really to grasp his melodic style, no mere listening is enough. The conscientious listener must sing.

But something can be accomplished by turning directly from the ricercar to the *Five Pieces for Orchestra,* Opus 10. Here is Webern's extreme originality, fully developed at the time of *Pierrot Lunaire* and the *Rite of Spring* (1912). The first piece of Opus 10 was written in 1911, and the others in 1913.

As in the Bach ricercar, here too every note is made clear and expressive by the instrumentation. Melodic motives are brought out by sharp contrasts. Again, even more here than in the Bach transcription, performers and listeners have to learn to feel the continuity from one melodic fragment to the next, and to recognize the subordination of one line to another. When this happens we know what Schoenberg meant, in his preface to Webern's Opus 9 (*Six Bagatelles for String Quartet*), by the phrase "a novel in every gesture." These melodies, amazingly enough, are symphonic. I have heard Opus 10, for instance, many times on the historic records of Robert Craft; further, I have heard the work when it was used as basis for a ballet, and again in a splendid concert conducted by Pierre Boulez. It is hard for me to recall that Webern's style once seemed to me *pointilliste,* if not quite insane.

When we turn to the *Symphony,* Opus 21, we find the same original style of instrumentation and melody, now extended into what for Webern is a very long span. Our study of the *Symphony* can be facilitated by twelve-tone analysis: it is a rewarding exercise to copy out the whole first movement on four staves in order to see the continuity of long lines, built out of the series and fragmented by instrumentation. But even without any such analysis, and without consideration of the canonic structure, so fascinating to Leland Smith,[12] it may be possible for sympathetic listeners to recognize and enjoy the marvelous form of this movement if their attention is drawn to certain harmonic features. One of these has been pointed out by many writers: the beginning uses the twelve notes in a remarkably narrow, symmetrical arrangement centered on A (Example 1). This structure pervades

Example 1. Webern, Symphony, Op. 21, analysis (first movement)

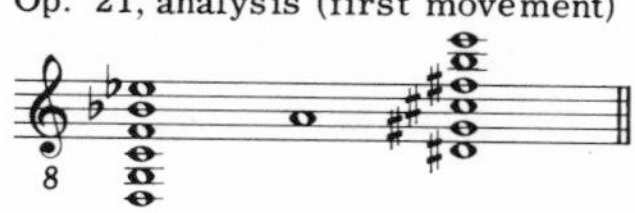

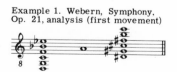

the whole exposition, which is repeated literally. The central A

[12] See "Composition and Precomposition in the Music of Webern," in this volume.

is the first note. The development section can be recognized by new, higher pitches, along with new rhythmic figures; its harmony is not quite symmetrical and not so narrowly limited in register, but rather dynamic (Example 2). Then comes the reca-

Example 2. Webern, Symphony, Op.21, analysis (first movement)

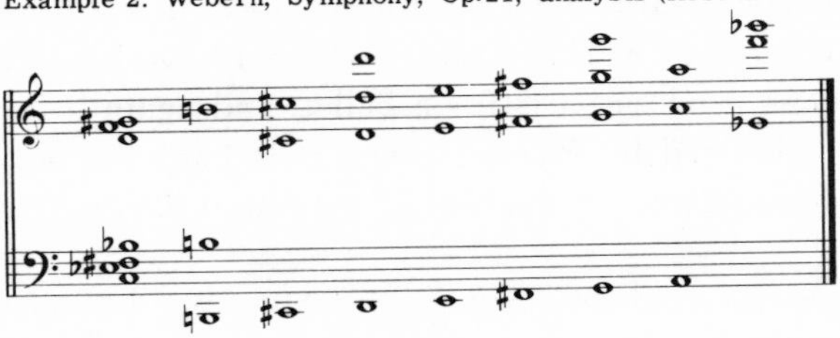

pitulation—hard to recognize because the melodies are so varied. The patient listener can discern, nevertheless, another symmetrical harmony, with these notes (Example 3):

Example 3. Webern, Symphony, Op. 21, analysis (first movement)

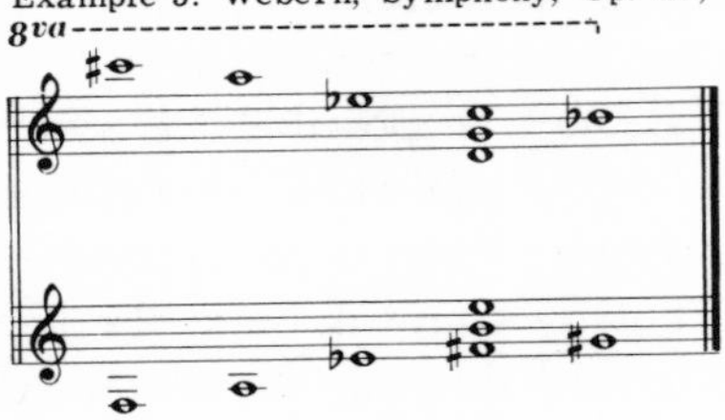

The original A below middle C is now reinforced by a brilliant overtone. A is no longer center, but rather almost like a frame.

This harmony, I believe, functions to articulate and unify the form of the movement. It is as characteristic of Webern as his instrumentation or his melody. Similar harmonic procedures can be found in several later works of his, while they differ profoundly from the procedures of Schoenberg, or Berg, or anyone else. Yet Webern shows here his relation to the tradition of form-building harmony in the symphonies of Haydn, Mozart, Beethoven, Brahms. Hearing this harmony in Webern's symphony clarifies and justifies the statements quoted above. It places him in the tradition of the symphony.

Webern modifies our sense of the tradition, as any true part of a tradition must do. He demands that we think again about Haydn, Mozart, and Beethoven, that we value their thematic contrasts less than their structural harmony, just as Sir Donald Tovey demands in his analytical essays.[13] This is contrary not only to Tchaikovsky and Shostakovich but also to Mahler and Schoenberg, for whom the contrasts of themes were extremely important—more so, I think, than any harmonic devices either old or new. Webern's symphony, naturally, does not displace Mahler and Schoenberg from the great tradition, but it shifts their places within it. Webern need not displace Sibelius or Shostakovich either, nor the very different works that Stravinsky composed in ignorance of Webern's works, such as the *Symphonies of Wind Instruments*, the *Symphony of Psalms*, and the *Symphony in Three Movements.* All of these still have an equal claim to "represent" our age, to point outward to future possibilities as varied as the past, and to serve as measuring points for contemporary efforts. We need not put Webern alone at the very center of the tradition. But we can see him as closer to the unknown center than to an extreme left wing. Through his symphony flows a precious connection between Beethoven and many of our contemporaries.

[13] D. F. Tovey, *Essays in Musical Analysis* (6 vols.; London, 1935-39).

LELAND SMITH

Composition and Precomposition in the Music of Webern

To the layman it often seems that a composer is completely free to write down any possible vocal or instrumental sounds in any combination whatsoever. To a certain extent this is a correct assumption, but in practice music has always been an art of many complex restrictions. These restrictions have operated at both the conscious and unconscious levels of composition. We might say that the unconscious restrictions are the cause of there being a "common practice" in a given era. The choice of a general style was not an act of free will for Mozart, but rather an acceptance of seemingly self-evident facts. Such restrictions might be called the precompositional attitude. However, at no time is there more than an ill-defined line between what is really left to the will of the composer and what is literally unthinkable for him either to do or not to do.

I doubt that Mozart ever "decided" to compose tonally. Rather, it seems likely that, despite some of his surprisingly complex tonal relationships, he would have found it unthinkable to produce something he could accept as music outside of the precepts of functional harmony. On the other hand, there were many things in eighteenth-century music of a precompositional nature that were dealt with in a fully conscious manner. First to come to mind is the idea of form. There were several formal schemes from which to choose; and, once this choice was made, a certain amount of the work of producing music was already done. I feel safe in assuming that, as a general rule, Mozart did not sit down at his desk, begin writing notes on paper, and then suddenly say to himself: "Ah, yes, these notes seem to fall into a key and make a tune that could very nicely open a symphony in G minor." But, of course, this does not rule out a composer's use of a sketchbook. The musical idea and its ideal environment need not come to mind simultaneously. However, most sketches of professional composers have been directed toward some particular work whose formal outlines are generally agreed upon by convention.

Other forms of conscious precomposition certainly have long played important roles in music. For example, almost as old as the idea of counterpoint itself is the recurrent desire of composers to produce multiplicity out of unity. The "common practice" at the end of the fifteenth century offered a particularly fertile field for this idea. In the mensuration canons of Ockeghem, Josquin, and others (which Webern knew so well), precomposition and composition seem to go hand in hand.

The precomposition consisted of the working out of single sets of horizontal relationships upon which an entire movement could be based. The creative element was entirely directed toward the establishment of a *system* that would "work out" right. Ideally, nothing was left to fancy, yet the results were to be aesthetically satisfying. Such a work is the "Agnus Dei" from Josquin's *Missa l'Homme Armé*. This movement bears the title *Ex una voce tres*, "out of one part come three." It was written as a single voice with three time signatures, showing its three voices to be performed in the ratios of 1:1, 2:1, and 3:1.

Moving ahead about two hundred years we can find somewhat similar precompositional procedures in Bach's *Musical Offering*. One of the sections consists of a cantus firmus (the "Royal Theme") and another line that includes two different clefs, one of which is upside down. Thus, by having one player read the music upside down and enter after the correct time lag, a canon by inversion is formed against the cantus firmus. (There is a remarkably similar passage in the first movement of Webern's *Quartet,* Opus 22, measures 6-15.)

In the music of earlier periods, many other elements might be subject to precompositional decision making. To mention a few: tonal relations between movements; which meter to adopt; instrumentation (for example, the use of brass meant something very different to Mozart from what it did to Bach); and so on. More might be said about the matter of instrumentation. The particular instrumental medium, once decided upon, usually remains a limiting factor. It is true that virtually all composers have at one time or another made transcriptions of some of their own works. But when the final product is truly intended to stand as a separate work of art, the composer (or, for that matter, any transcriber) must, in a sense, recompose the work to fit the new precompositional demands. Beethoven wrote as follows about his arrangement of the *Piano Sonata* in E, Opus 14, No. 1, as a *Quartet* in F:

> Not only would whole passages have to be entirely omitted or altered, but some would have to be added; and there one finds the nasty stumbling-block, to overcome which one must either be the composer himself or at any rate possess the same skill and inventiveness.[1]

It might be mentioned in passing that some twentieth-century composers have apparently refused to be limited by their original decisions on instrumentation. Honegger added a trumpet to the finale of his *Symphony No. 2 for String Orchestra;* and Ives added a flute and viola to his *Second Piano Sonata* ("Concord Sonata").

The list of precompositional elements could be extended to include virtually everything that went into the "common practice" of an era. What, then, was left to composition? Almost every-

[1] *The Letters of Beethoven,* collected, translated, and edited by Emily Anderson (3 vols.; London: Macmillan Co.; New York: St. Martin's Press, 1961), I, 75.

thing, in the sense that a composer such as Mozart found many possible sound combinations inconceivable as music, and that his conscious precompositional choices did no more than create a frame of reference for his imagination. Thus, Mozart was free to write a passage near the end of *Don Giovanni* of such chromaticism that it could be taken by Darius Milhaud as the twelve-tone basis for a scene in his opera *David,* because Mozart's use of this material in no way violates the precepts of functional harmony.

In his *Poetics of Music,* Igor Stravinsky has beautifully expressed himself on the subject of precompositional restrictions:

> My freedom thus consists in my moving about within the narrow frame that I have assigned myself for each one of my undertakings. I shall go even farther: my freedom will be so much the greater and more meaningful the more narrowly I limit my field of action. . . . The more constraints one imposes, the more one frees one's self of the chains that shackle the spirit.[2]

At first glance, there seems to be very little "common practice" in the twentieth century. But perhaps we are misled somewhat by the fact that most contemporary composers do not tend to "sound" as alike as, say, Haydn and Mozart do. In fact, Stravinsky's *Piano Concerto* and his *Movements for Piano and Orchestra* "sound" more different from each other to many ears than do Wagner's Prelude to *Die Meistersinger* and Mozart's Overture to the *Magic Flute.* And yet, if we compare the apparent precompositional attitude of Stravinsky in the 1920's with Stravinsky in the 1960's, we find the same feeling about the need for the definition of limits. The context for each work must be established anew. This is not to say that everything to be used in an individual work must derive its meaning from relationships entirely within that work. Rather, when well-understood musical items from the past are used out of their original context, they

[2] Igor Stravinsky, *Poetics of Music in the Form of Six Lessons,* translated by Arthur Knodel and Ingolf Dahl (Cambridge, Mass.: Harvard University Press, 1947), p. 65.

still retain strong references to that earlier context, regardless of the completely new surroundings. Thus the total context of a new work inevitably includes all such external references, no matter how much at odds they may be with other elements of the context.

In the twentieth century, contextuality has replaced tonality (i.e., functional harmony) as the basic precompositional attitude. The present-day composer who does not consciously or otherwise set up a special set of materials and methods for his work finds himself in a vast uncharted sea of possibilities. Today it would be just as unthinkable for a sophisticated musician to embark upon a new work without some clear idea of a special context, even if it is a completely negative idea, as it would have been for Mozart to begin composing without reference to a key.

The twelve-tone technique represented the first important attempt at a systematic solution to the problems raised by contextuality. While the general concept of serial technique (whether twelve-tone or non-twelve-tone) seems to be somewhat applicable to most nontonal twentieth-century music, I prefer the term *contextual* as being descriptive of our "common practice." It broadly represents procedures of which the twelve-tone system, serial technique, partly tonal referential practices, and perhaps even controlled or free improvisation are special cases. In all these cases the primary basis for organization, and hence the framework within which "musical meaning" is created, is the interaction of the various elements that are presented by the special context.

All but the earliest works of Webern are organized primarily from the contextual point of view. Beginning with Opus 17, the pitch-interval relations came to be organized according to twelve-tone procedures. However, even in Opus 1 and Opus 2, two of the most direct methods of contextual organization—variation and canon—contribute as much to musical unity on all levels as does tonality per se. It might be said that the use of tonality in these two works was unconscious, since in 1908 it was still only barely thinkable to produce music beyond tonal references. The potential of tonality for multiplicity of function and ambiguity had reached its climax by the end of the nineteenth century. It rapidly became clear that if music was to continue to make vital use of the materials of the immediate past, the relations of motive and interval would have to take over as the prime organizational bases. The earliest contextual movements were almost all quite short. With the requirements of motivic unity, and without the possibility of clear contrasts of tonality, it was difficult to extend a movement beyond the working-out of a single idea. Transpositions, rhythmic transformations, and so forth, were already part of the basic fabric, and thus of no great use in extending the formal units.

Schoenberg's practical applications of the twelve-tone technique opened up new possibilities for the meaningful extension of musical movements. Through a finer definition of the intervallic bases of each musical context, the composer was free to develop and contrast his material in terms which were undreamt of twenty years earlier.

Webern was the first composer of importance to dedicate himself fully and without reservation to the twelve-tone technique. While it was certainly conceivable for Webern, after 1924, to write in other modes of contextual expression, there is no evidence that he ever seriously considered doing so. Thus, the use of the twelve-tone technique became for him as axiomatic as was the use of tonality for Mozart.

Just before the twelve-tone system became available to Webern, he apparently felt the need for some more precise organizational principle than free motivic contextuality. Foremost, and perhaps simplest, among the extradodecaphonic contextual devices is the canon. Canons play no important role in Webern's music after Opus 2 until we reach the last song of Opus 15 and the *Five Canons,* Opus 16. The sketches for Opus 16 in the Moldenhauer Archive reveal just how much work went into the creation of Webern's exquisite miniatures. The precompositional element of strict devotion to the canon is of course clear. Less strict, but perhaps a factor of equal importance to the final sound of the music, is Webern's consistent use of interval combinations which are as far from the simple harmonic functions as possible. The half step with octave displacement is set forth as a kind of standard of melodic and harmonic relationship. Virtually every phrase cell in the work prominently features this element. (In fact, the final leaps in the last canon each cover two octaves plus a half step.) It is possible that there was a certain negative quality in this; that is, that the composer wished never to give the listener any opportunity to imagine a tonal harmonic function. Be that as it may, this precompositional decision was always put to decidedly positive contextual use by composers of talent.

When we study Webern's sketches, we see that the particular notes and rhythms used in the *Five Canons* are precompositionally determined only insofar as the leading voice is carefully contrived to generate harmonic combinations that are consistent with the melodic intervals. It is plain to see that Webern was not easily satisfied when composing these works. The sketches show many different versions—in fact, there are seven pages devoted to just one twelve-bar piece.

To oversimplify, it might be said that the real composition in these canons consisted merely of finding one possible leading voice for each piece. Beyond this, there were left only what Schumann called the items of secondary composition, such as the tempo, dynamics, and so on—and Webern left these in a rather vague state until the final versions. Summarizing in regard to the *Five Canons,* Opus 16, we may say that the precompositional decisions determined what the standards and process of composition would be. Any notes and rhythms could be used, so long as they made a positive contribution to each work's context—a context that was continually in a state of evolution as it was being established, while remaining always under the control of the precompositional dictums.

Webern's first twelve-tone works represented a return to the quasimotivic contextual basis that characterized most of his earlier works. Generally, it seems that the order of the twelve pitches is of hardly greater import than the fact that the total repertory of pitch classes is continually being unfolded, thus helping to insure the avoidance of tonality. In the *String Trio,* Opus 20, Webern begins to become aware of the new potential to be found in the tone row. His use of set sequences of row forms in this work adds a new dimension to nontonal musical expression. These row sequences are certainly not mere substitutions for tonal functions. But in one sense they serve the same purpose, in that certain larger standards of relationship are clearly set forth. The form may be extended through literal repetition of the row-form relationships, while at the same time the important quality of detail is maintained.

The particular row Webern chose for Opus 20 actually contains much potential that was left unrealized (Example 1). The series is

Example 1. Webern, tone row for String Trio, Op. 20

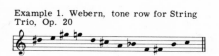

made up of six half-step units, separated from each other by a major third or perfect fourth. This structure makes possible extensive overlapping of rows, and double function of intervals. However, it is not until Opus 21 that such elements are incorporated into the musical result.

The *Symphony,* Opus 21, marks Webern's first great extension of precomposition into some of the areas normally left open to freer treatment. The opening section of the first movement offers not only a strict double canon, but also a strict placement of the pitches so that there are only 13 positions for the 144 (i.e., 12 × 12) row notes used. Likewise, all the notes used are located to form a pattern that centers on the first A and spreads by equidistant intervals from that point (Example 2). The middle part of the

Example 2. Webern, Symphony, Op. 21, analysis of opening section, first movement

movement is a four-part canon that is restated in retrograde. Here the pitches are equidistantly arranged from an E in the upper two parts, and from a B flat in the lower parts (Example 3). The final double canon returns to the original row forms of the opening,

Example 3. Webern, Symphony, Op. 21, analysis of middle section, first movement

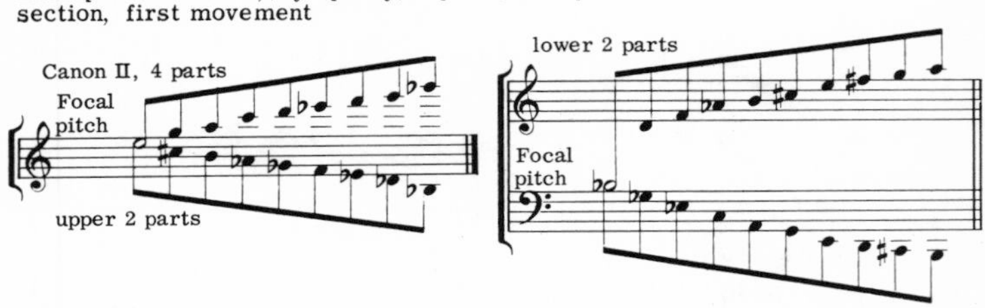

but now at a much higher range and with the notes arranged to center on E and D (Example 4).

When we consider that the note falling between the last two named, i.e., the implied focal pitch, is E flat, another kind of pattern emerges: Canon I, focal pitch A; Canon II, focal pitches E,

Example 4. Webern, Symphony, Op. 21, analysis of final double canon, first movement

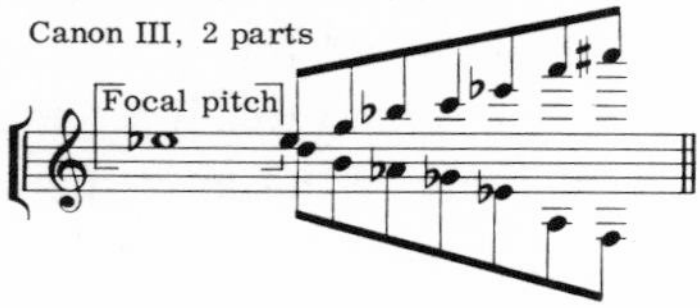

B flat; Canon III, focal pitch E flat. Thus, the organization of the original form of the row becomes a factor of the largest structure (Example 5).

Example 5. Webern, Symphony, Op. 21, tone row (basic set) in relation to structure, first movement

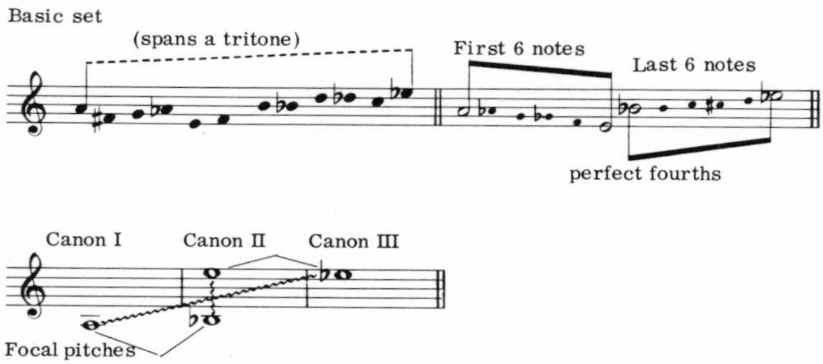

Of further interest is the fact that the row form of the leading voice of the middle canon also spans the interval E–B flat, or a perfect fifth (with octave shifts) above the level of Canons I and III. The over-all form, as summarized in Example 6, implies—repeats and all!—a strong musical reference to Baroque binary form:

||: Tonic . . . Dominant :**||**: Dominant . . . Tonic :**||**

Example 6. Webern, Symphony, Op. 21, over-all form, first movement

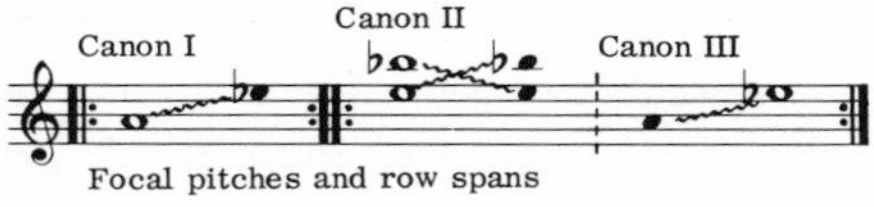

The second movement (theme, seven variations, coda) grows out of a somewhat wider variety of precompositional processes. At the same time, the overt use of the variation principle makes this movement seem much more rigid than the first one. Although the tempi may vary, all nine sections of the movement have the same number of bars, eleven ($9 \times 11 = 99$ in all), and each eleven-bar section is divided in half, the two halves in some sense forming mirror images of each other. While the "sound" may vary considerably, each of the first four sections has its "procedural" counterpart among the last four sections, and these are arranged to form an arch with the fifth part (i.e., Variation IV), the only unique section, at its center (Example 7). Almost overnight, in

Example 7. Webern, Symphony, Op. 21, over-all form, second movement

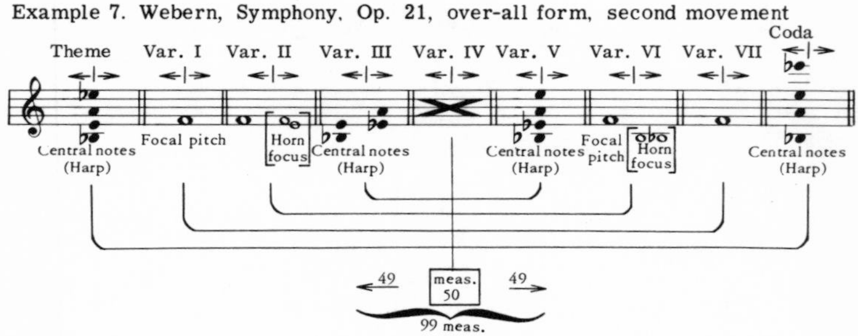

this work, Webern seemed to become aware of the vast possibilities of large-scale precompositional planning with the twelve-tone technique.

The *Quartet* with saxophone, Opus 22, incorporates many of the features already seen in the *Symphony*. What is missing is the austere strictness that pervades the *Symphony*. In the first movement of the *Quartet*, the tone rows are again treated canonically, but now with a refreshing rhythmic freedom. There are tiny cells of two or three notes that are given rhythmic identity, but the negative space—the rests between the cells—is constantly changing size. At the beginning, the second voice of the canon follows at the distance of a quarter rest. In the second cell, the second voice now leads the first by the distance of an eighth rest; then this space is reduced to a sixteenth as we are led into the delicious repeated F sharp of the clarinet (where the two row forms meet). In the last cell, the second voice again trails, now by a sixteenth. This kind of procedure becomes a norm for the movement. The very relaxed quality of the individual cells is enhanced by this somewhat free attitude toward the rhythmic relationship between the cells.

This is all beautifully balanced, however, by a strictness of twelve-tone procedure, the use of closed-form repeats, and a high degree of symmetry in the arrangement of pitches. Once more Webern has chosen a row that spans the tritone. But now the first or last row notes are not prominent as centers of symmetrical arrangements; more often, notes from the middle of the series play this role. The various row combinations are planned so that the notes C and F sharp are the meeting points of each set of two rows (Example 8). The two row forms found at the opening and

Example 8. Webern, Quartet with Saxophone, Op. 22, analysis, first movement

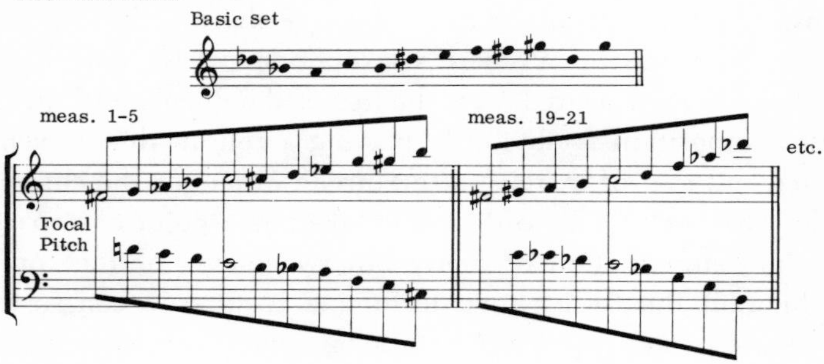

close of the movement span the intervals C sharp–G and B–F, thus straddling the emphasized C and F sharp. (Also note that the other movement of the *Quartet* begins with C and F sharp, and ends with a solo F sharp by the saxophone.) All the notes in the first movement center on the F sharp, except for those of a cantus firmus type of line first presented by the saxophone in measures 6 to 15. I might also point out that this cantus firmus is the only part of the movement that is not party to any of the canons.

From the formal point of view, we have here a movement that displays a very real relation to the early classic sonata, although this relation would be even closer if Webern had included the first five bars in his first repeat. In the "development" section, the climax is reached by extending outward from the focal F sharp to the tritone-related C, two and a half octaves in each direction. Then, when the focal F sharp is once more reached, we are into the abbreviated and retrograde recapitulation of the opening of the movement. A summary of the form follows:

meas.	1-5	6-15	16-24	24-27	28-37	37-44
	A	‖: B a :‖	‖: "development"	A, retrograde	B a :‖	Coda
		(Saxophone "cantus firmus")	(A')	(recapitulation)	("cantus firmus")	(A")

Apart from the aforementioned cantus firmus, I find this movement to be highly reminiscent of the famous figure study by Leonardo da Vinci (1453-1519) in which man's extremities are shown to be equidistant from his navel. F sharp is the "navel" of the first movement of Webern's saxophone quartet, and the high and low C's in measure 22 are the tips of the fingers and the toes.

Precomposition is obviously playing a role in this movement far beyond that of merely setting up an order for the chromatic scale. The twelve-tone ordering is taken as a point of departure for the determination of many other elements of the context. Nothing in the twelve-tone technique requires a composer to make use of symmetrical formations, canons, closed form—or, for that matter, even the presentation of all twelve notes before one is repeated (as some students seem to be taught). The composer must decide, in advance, regarding what aspects of the twelve-tone technique are to be utilized, and how they might be related to the contextual total.

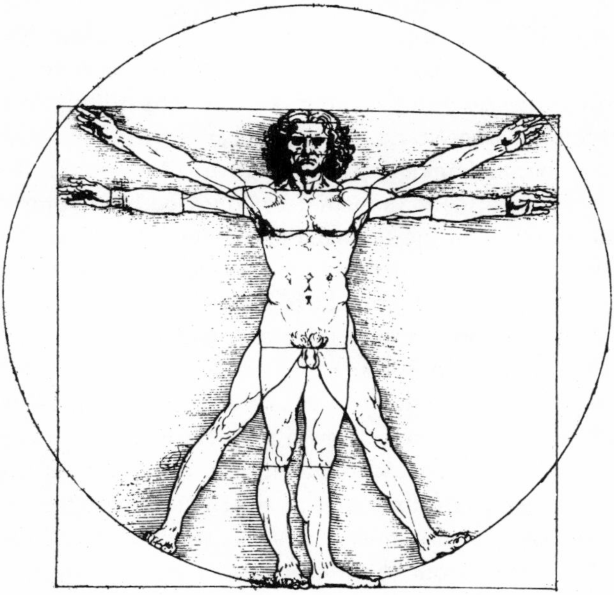

The other movement of this quartet marks an abrupt shift away from such a multitude of precompositional procedures. I have already mentioned that C and F sharp are the prominent beginning and ending notes, but this movement has no "navel," and canonic action is rarely heard for more than a couple of bars at a time. Nevertheless, a kind of rondo (or even sonata-rondo) structure comes to view upon analysis of the row forms utilized. This is certainly not as audible as the form of the first movement, but then it is clear that Webern wished to produce a completely different effect in the finale.

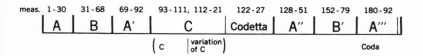

meas.	1-30	31-68	69-92	93-111, 112-21	122-27	128-51	152-79	180-92
	A	B	A′	C	Codetta	A″	B′	A‴
				(c | variation of C)				Coda

The primary element of this rondo is virtually athematic. Its recurrences are marked mainly by the use of row forms that begin and end on C and F sharp—and the frequent overlappings with other row forms tend to obscure even this. The middle section (C in the diagram) does stand in relief because of the persistent use of a quiet parallel major-seventh figure. Once more it is not easy to hear that this is immediately followed by a complex and energetic variation of the same material, which then leads through a *pesante* codetta and into a highly varied recapitulation of the movement's opening. The coda is made up of short, rapid explosions of notes in extreme registers, and then the movement ends with a quiet solo F sharp.

In most of Webern's later work, more of the details tended to be controlled by precomposition than were left to free composition. The framework, which in twentieth-century music had always been much more than just an abstraction that might apply to many different pieces, now almost became the piece itself. The famous "scherzo" from the *Variations,* Opus 27, for piano, is such a movement. The order, location, and groupings of the notes, as well as the large phrase structure, are highly regulated. Only the rests, and sequences of dynamics and phrasing, seem to have been composed rather than precomposed. However, the lack of symmetry in these latter items only serves to heighten the ear's awareness of the precomposed elements.

A very different kind of piece is *Das Augenlicht,* Opus 26. The tone rows are all finally completed, but often in such a manner as to be completely inaudible; there are many canonic passages, but they often break down into free imitation; row forms are combined into units of great potential, but nothing special seems to come of them. Still, the work is of unquestionable beauty. Here the contextual basis is considerably broader than that found in some of the other music discussed. The aesthetic effect of a piece like *Das Augenlicht* is bound to be different from that of a piece like the *Symphony,* but the value of each is increased by the existence of the other.

For some years the precomposed quality in Webern's music was the major source of inspiration for many of the most talented younger composers. There was (and remains) much of great value to learn from Webern's special contribution to this field. But interest in *total* precomposition now seems to be rapidly waning. It has become apparent that total control and total chance effectively occupy the same point on the orbit of expressive values. Both procedures tend to dehumanize the art of music and make it into a mere phenomenon. Real composers are always discovering anew what Webern knew so well: that no one particular balance of precomposition and composition is superior to any other; and that, in any case, the impact of art depends always on the obvious presence of human intent.

ERNST KRENEK

New Dimensions of Music

Anton von Webern was not a theorist of music. Unlike Schoenberg, he did not seem to feel the urge to organize his ideas on music as a consistent and comprehensive intellectual edifice. From his analytical utterances[1] we can see that he was quite conscious of what he was doing as a composer, and his compositions, especially the later ones, could never have been written without a remarkable amount of keen ratiocination. However, his verbalization of these intellectual processes remained curiously obtuse, as if he had been struggling with some inhibitions that prevented him from becoming fully articulate.

Thus the contemporary composers who so confidently elected Webern to be their guide into the unknown took their cues from his creative work rather than from any theoretical statements. They were particularly attracted by Webern's foreshadowing a more generalized application of the serial principle than that practiced in the "classical" twelve-tone technique up to 1950. Significant groundwork had been laid by the French composer, Olivier Messiaen, who had published a treatise dealing with preformed rhythmic patterns. It was for students of Messiaen, such as his compatriot, Pierre Boulez, and the German, Karlheinz Stockhausen, to pursue this idea systematically and to combine

[1] See those I have quoted in "Anton von Webern: A Profile," in this volume.

the concept of the twelve-tone row (a prearranged pattern of pitches) with that of the time row (a prearranged pattern of durations). This was well in keeping with the basic philosophy of the twelve-tone technique, its ethical *raison d'être,* so to speak, which put special emphasis on integration of the constituent elements of a musical process by deriving all of them from one single nucleus, that is, from the single, freely chosen pitch pattern of the tone row.

The first attempts at setting up time rows related to the tone row were somewhat elementary. Thus, for instance, Boulez, in his *Structures I,* simply assigned to each tone of his pitch series a time value, from one to twelve sixteenth-notes long. As the tones would appear throughout the work in the manner established in the "classical" twelve-tone technique, the time values would automatically parallel the varying combinations of their associate pitches and thus provide a fairly complex rhythmic picture. Later, much more elaborate methods were invented in order to derive time patterns from the basic tone rows.

The essential problem is to extract from the tone row a set of numerical magnitudes which can be used in the computation of time values and to organize these in some proportional relations, which, of course, must in turn be derived from the basic set, and so on all the way to the over-all structural design of the whole work. The most obvious point of departure for deriving numerical magnitudes from the tone row is the intervals between the consecutive tones of the row, since their sizes can be measured: either in terms of ratios of the frequencies encompassing the intervals (a process described and applied by Stockhausen), or by counting the half-steps between the two limiting tones of the interval (a method preferred by this writer and by other composers, among whom the American, Milton Babbitt, deserves special mention, since he is one of the first composers anywhere to base a composition on serially integrated predetermination of pitch order and time order).

If this sounds like specious trivia in no way related to the spontaneous outflow of emotional expression which is supposed to be the real concern of a true composer, it ought to be realized that introduction of serial thinking has intensely affected the character of music altogether, so that modes of reception and response are also undergoing considerable changes. While in the twelve-tone technique only the succession of pitches was prearranged, so that the composer remained free in his treatment of other variables (such as time, density of texture, dynamics, timbre), expansion of the serial principle over these sectors resulted in complete predetermination of all musical happenings. This in turn eliminated the formation of those musical shapes that were known as "themes" and the progressive variations thereof which were called "development." Thus the traditional forms of music, such as rondo, sonata, and others, went overboard, too. Obviously music based on such totally different premises suggests a change of orientation and receptive expectation on the part of the listener.

It appears likely that the younger composers who turned to serial techniques around 1950 were strongly motivated by the promise of emancipation from traditional structural models, adherence to which had still prevailed in much of the dodecaphonic writing of the preceding generation. These older composers, after having exploited the possibilities of integrating the twelve-tone technique with earlier concepts, became interested in modifying the basic elements of this technique and in experimenting with the application of the serial idea to other aspects than those of pitch.

One of the modifications which I should like to mention as an example, because it appeared to me to be most significant, was the idea of rotation. I applied it as early as 1941 in my choral work, *Lamentatio Jeremiae Prophetae,* and later, with increasing consequence, in other works. This principle consists in systematic and serially determined progressive switching of tones within the chosen row. It turned out to be of paramount importance in my essays in serial writing because the continuous combination of constant (invariant) elements with systematically (serially) varying elements produces the desirable degree of unpredictable surprise.

Composers of serial music became interested in the electronic medium, which through the improvement of sound-generating devices and of tape-recording methods began to offer serious compositional potentialities at about the same time as the serial concept took hold of the composers' imagination. While it is entirely possible to arrange electronic sounds to fit any stylistic image, the serial composers were attracted to the medium by its capacity for producing sound qualities otherwise unobtainable (such as would be adequate to the newness of the substance of serial music). Furthermore, the mechanics of electronic production and recording of sound made available an extraordinary degree of accuracy, which was an answer to the problems raised by the increasing rhythmic intricacy of serial music.

The propensity for extreme timbres, noticeable especially in early atonal music (which includes Webern's sets of orchestral pieces), is due not so much to the desire for a wealth of hues and shadings so characteristic of impressionistic music as to the urge to articulate the design with utmost clarity. In recent serial (and "postserial") music the interest in unusual timbres produced by new-fangled instruments or by playing on the traditional ones in odd manners has increased to an extent that frequently seems to revive the ways of impressionistic imagination. Undoubtedly this tendency was enhanced by the experience of the unheard-of sonorities of the electronic medium.

While the notion of mathematically supported predetermination and rigorously pursued accuracy of execution implies complete rational control of the minutest details, paradoxically this very principle opens the door to its ostensible opposite, to the element of chance. The explanation is twofold. Predetermination of certain "parameters" (or variables) automatically excludes other parameters from similar determination, because whatever happens in their sectors has already been decided by the primary regulations. To give a very elementary example: if, in a polyphonic piece of two or more voices, the prearranged tone row indicates in what succession pitches should enter the process, and the prearranged time series prescribes when they should enter, we cannot any longer try to set up a similar prearrangement for the harmonies, or chords, that will emerge from the simultaneous progress of the voices. In this sector we shall have to accept what we get as a result of our previous operations. Thus these sound combinations are implicitly prearranged too, but, since we could not consciously calculate them like the first two parameters, we cannot safely predict what they will be, and in that respect we might consider them chance results.

Second, music of this kind has no generally accepted and familiar framework, such as the tonal idiom, the standardized phrase construction, and the set structures of traditional music, all of which caused the listener to entertain certain expectations as to what course in broad lines a piece of music would presumably take. In serial music each work is the result of individual programing, and the programs are not self-revealing as they were in traditional music, when the first few bars disclosed a piece to be, let us say, in A major, so that whatever happened in that piece could be related to the known set of assumptions implied in the definition of A major. Thus, in the view of many listeners serial music appears to be a sequence of chance happenings.

In recent developments the factor of chance has gained increasing significance in various ways. In the first place, the ancient concept of improvisation was revived in that composers would grant the interpreters certain liberties in dealing with the *res prius facta,* the written composition, whose structural components could be played in different successions, varied in speed and articulation, according to the whims of the interpreter. In other cases, the composer would indicate the general stylistic and structural framework of his musical conceit and leave it to the interpreters to fill various only vaguely delineated areas with sound combinations of their own, presumably congenial, invention. Frequently such a vague delineation consists of elaborate graphic designs which do not any longer resemble musical notation, but rather look like a pictorial representation suggestive of the general character of the music imagined by the composer, like a translation of its aural image into the visual medium.

Finally, the compositional process itself becomes the object of chance operations when the selection and placement of tones is decided by transferring totally extraneous graphic patterns (such as the dots depicting the locations of stars on a celestial map) onto music paper, by throwing dice or consulting oracle books. John Cage and a group of his followers have pioneered in this field.

In these developments, a direct influence of Webern may hardly be verified. The assertion, voiced by some of the "progressives," that these innovations signify the demise of serial music, is neither demonstrable nor relevant. Just as the twelve-tone technique was constantly reviewed, revised, reshaped, remodeled, and applied in countless varying situations without ever being abandoned, so will the serial concepts govern musical thinking for a long time to come, even if their application should be still less obvious than it has been so far. Undoubtedly Anton von Webern will continue to be recognized as the fountainhead of this kind of musical thinking.

EGON WELLESZ

Anton von Webern, a Great Austrian

Of those who belonged to the first group of pupils of Arnold Schoenberg when he began teaching in Vienna, I am now the only one left. Moreover, I had links outside this circle with Anton von Webern since we both studied at the University of Vienna and went to the Musikhistorisches Institut of Professor Guido Adler. Here it was, in October, 1904, that we used to meet and play together on the piano the *Third Symphony* of Mahler, which was to be performed that season. We went together to all the rehearsals which Mahler conducted of that symphony and, in later years, to those of the *Fifth Symphony* and the *Sixth Symphony*. In Professor Adler's seminar we played Beethoven's last quartets on the piano and analyzed them.

Working together, attending the same concerts and the same operas, and, above all, studying with Schoenberg—all this created a bond that was to survive the years at the university and the different courses our lives were to take. From then onward a comradeship developed that continued until I left Vienna in 1938. Then came the war, and for Webern the destruction of all that he had cherished.

The death of an artist, of a poet, a composer, sometimes produces a miracle: he suddenly appears "*au dessus de la mêlée.*" How great a change we witness in the case of Anton Webern! Fifty years ago every performance of one of his works raised to the boiling point the fury of his opponents and of the music critics. The few fanatical adherents, on the other hand, broke out into boisterous cheers, but they were unable to stem the hostile tide. However, in the days before World War I—here I speak from my own experience—and even in postwar days, while Schoenberg's Verein für musikalische Privataufführungen existed, Webern never showed signs of being depressed or unhappy at the lack of recognition. We were all used to being ignored by the official circles in Vienna, and ridiculed and attacked by nearly all the music critics. We all believed in Mahler's famous dictum: "I run with my head against the wall, but it is the wall which will crack."

Webern found an outlet in his activity as a conductor of the Arbeiter Konzerte, and as chairman of the Vienna section of the International Music Society.

It is my sincere hope that, before it is too late, a chronicler may be found to record how much Vienna owed to Webern, in the years between the wars, for his activities in maintaining the contact with contemporary music, while those whose duty it was to keep up these contacts failed to fulfill their obligations. The lights went out for Webern when Schoenberg left Europe and Berg died. From then on he seems to have walked in a dark cloud. The last message I received was a postcard in the late summer of 1939. It began: *"Ja, mein Lieber, es ist ganz anders gekommen, als wir uns es vorgestellt haben"* ("Yes, my dear fellow, things have taken a turn quite different from what we had expected"). For him the dark cloud did not disperse and vanish with the end of the war. His end came like the inevitable death of the hero in a tragedy.

There is, to my mind, one lesson which the younger generation should learn from Webern: the wide range of his taste, not only in the music of the past but, more significantly, in contemporary music. For him only one criterion existed in judging a composition: he must feel that what was expressed was true. Let me give one example. When we first met, Webern was strongly impressed by Richard Strauss; Mahler's music did not appeal to him. However, as soon as he had grasped its profound sincerity, Mahler's music, so opposed to his own, grew on him and he became one of its most enthusiastic exponents.

This same criterion of truth must be applied to Webern's own music. It is not its novelty, its construction, its elaborate twelve-tone technique that make it so "remarkable"—to use the word in its old sense. It is the uncompromising sincerity of Webern's music that gives it so prominent a place in our time.

This is the portrait of Webern that I have carried with me since the days of our youth. He was one of the last musicians of a great tradition—a great Austrian, and fully aware of this spiritual inheritance, like Rainer Maria Rilke and like his favorite poet Georg Trakl. An Austrian, who knew all the obstacles, all the enmities, all the jealousies to which he was exposed by living and working in Vienna, but in spite of all that, carried on, saying "*dennoch*" ("nevertheless"). He was aware that fame would come only after his death—and so it was. Fame came abundantly when the book of life was closed.

CESAR BRESGEN

Webern's Last Months in Mittersill

It was in the last four months of Anton von Webern's life that by a strange chance I became his neighbor in Mittersill—the neighbor of the modest house "Burg 31" into which Webern had moved on his flight from Vienna. The rooms were as humble as could be, but hospitable. They overlooked a path of open fields bounded by steeply graded mountain slopes; even in the depth of summer a frosty breath from the gleaming snowfields penetrated to the valley.

When, in May of 1945, a few days before the capitulation, I first visited Webern, he gave the impression of grave illness. He had stomach trouble, and almost every means for real treatment was lacking. And yet Webern recovered relatively quickly from all his recent hardships, the months-long deprivations and concerns. The atmosphere of the high mountain air restored Webern visibly, as he himself admitted. It was like a real breath of relief, which expressed itself, too, in the fact that he resumed the thought of future creation. It seems certain that Webern committed no works to paper at that time. Yet I still remember distinctly that he was repeatedly busy at a shabby little table with pencil and compass, occupied with geometrical figures or lines and signs. He explained to me once, too, that he no longer needed to hear his work performed; the work sounded "in itself"—he himself could hear it completely with his inner ear. Once it was committed to notation, if only on the bare tabletop, Webern deemed the real work completed. "The sound is always there," he said; a rendition could by no means recreate it so perfectly. In other words, Webern was then living more and more in a tonal realm of ideas which—and this seems to me important—he not only calculated in advance, but could actually hear.

From time to time one would see Webern walking alone in the wonderful evergreen forests above the Castle Mittersill; there one finds broad forest floors with a rich carpeting of moss and fascinating glimpses of the Hohen Tauern. In this lonely period I liked to go mushroom hunting, and occasionally my path crossed Webern's. One evening, about ten days before Webern's death, has remained especially in my memory. The master admired the contents of my well-filled basket, in which lay some rare and interesting mushrooms. Obviously stirred by the sight, he spoke admiringly of the rich variety of forms in nature. We fell to contemplating the remarkable qualities of fungi, mosses, and lichens, and I still remember that point in our conversation at which Webern broke off to scrutinize a curious lichen that had so covered a large stone that it looked like an etching. This extraordinary veined network both moved one to reflection and was somehow touching: after all, it was a part of life, growing organically according to a design, indebted to a higher and hidden reason.

Webern's very touching joy in the little wonders of nature, especially in the world of vegetation, was known to all who came close to him. Characteristic was the long contemplation of things, the immersion of himself in them; thus, when he observed a fern or a mountain flower, it was preferably in its habitat. And what a habitat that was! This Mittersill, close to the main crest of the Hohen Tauern, offers quite unusual contrasts of landscape. Those last ten days before Webern's death especially were filled with a late summer luminosity of a radiant nature: early snow on the northern slopes, but on those exposed to the sun still real summer, and a sky above as blue as it can only be in the high mountains.

This purity of color, as well as the peace that emanates from that harmonious valley scene, with its old peasant houses and churches, never failed to delight Webern. In the last days of his life he must have felt this peace intensely, for the days were unusually serene and harmonious.

At this time we also had a conversation about Gregorian chant. One must bear in mind that it is scarcely possible to speak of any real Gregorian tradition in such places in Austria. The church choirs content themselves with the usual *Landmessen*, polyphonic jetsam of the nineteenth century. But I made the attempt, with the church choir then entrusted to me at Mittersill, to introduce at early mass a certain amount of Gregorian chant. Webern took especial delight in this, so that several times he appeared at such an early mass. Not only was he a considerable connoisseur of Gregorian chant, but he esteemed it altogether highly. After one such mass he said: "At last a pure line once more, this glorious monody. . . . It is quintessential music, complete in itself." It may at first seem surprising that Webern had such a pronounced affinity for monody; but, if one enters more deeply into the question, it becomes clear that there are certain connections between the musical logic of Webern and the structure of Gregorian chant. Their common root is melodic thinking, though of course with a vast differentiation.

No one would have thought that just a few days after this conversation a Gregorian mass would be the last music to envelop Webern's mortal remains. In the plain little Baroque church at Mittersill, five persons followed the progress of that Requiem mass sung by the celebrant Dean Ehrenstrasser, his assistant, and myself. Outside there was again that radiant sky, and early snow lay on the mountains. Quietly, and unspoiled by noisy or impure distractions, this hour produced a lasting impression in the memory. Beyond the churchyard wall, people passed as always: townsfolk, peasants, children, soldiers of the Occupation, refugees, and beggars. But beside the open grave stood the five persons, and sought consolation in the rite, fulfilled, as it has ever been in all times, by the priest and his assistants. If ever, then in such an hour, was revealed not only the meaning but the efficacy of the ancient prayers, which must also touch all those who, far away and apart, ever bring to mind the memory of the dead master.

I cannot conclude these remarks without recollecting gratefully the tolerance that was ingrained in Webern and that never failed to amaze—a tolerance toward other contemporaries as well as past epochs and masters. Two or three times Webern attended the little recitals held in our neighboring abode. A violinist, who also had found his way hither as a refugee from Vienna, and I shared the modest programs: old classics, Mozart, perhaps Hindemith and Debussy—nothing more was to be expected. Webern came as a grateful listener. At the performance of my own works he expressed an alert but never wounding criticism. The formulation of his judgment was terse but never dispiriting. Of course, he proceeded from the premise that a completely new development of music would now begin. The future composer would, however, grasp this "newness" of his own accord, would "breathe this fresh morning air and absorb it as a matter of course." "In fifty years at the most," he said, "everyone will experience this music as *their* innate music; yes, even for children it will be accessible . . . people will sing it."[1] Despite this firm conviction, this lofty self-assurance, Webern in our conversations, at which my mother was sometimes also present, did not ridicule contemporaries who thought otherwise, nor did he call the old, bad or inferior. He himself had access to every kind of genuine art, but he was keenly aware of the necessity for sharp differentiation of the new, if the new was truly to form a whole. There could be no compromises for Webern; but respect for those who thought differently distinguished him and determined his image as a man. It is an image of

[1] *"In spätestens 50 Jahren werden alle Menschen diese Musik als* i h r e *natürliche Musik erleben, ja selbst den Kindern wird sie zugänglich sein . . . man wird sie singen."*

goodness, of modesty, but at the same time of awareness of what is transitory, of suffering, and of renunciation.

Yet, in conversation, this image was intensified by a pride born of his conviction of the rightness of his new musical standpoint, and the permanence of his thought in the sense of a doctrine. Then the countenance of the man would light up in a strange way, such as is accorded only to those who know ultimate truth.

HANS MOLDENHAUER

A Webern Archive in America

INTRODUCTION

The Pacific Northwest of the United States of America, some seven thousand miles distant from Anton von Webern's native Vienna, might appear an unlikely place for the establishment of an archive for primary source materials of and about a composer who throughout his life remained deeply rooted in Austrian soil. Yet, a chain of interlacing circumstances has brought about just such a phenomenon.

The history of the Webern Archive began with a chance visit to Mittersill in 1959 and the ensuing impulse to conduct an inquiry into the circumstances of Webern's tragic death in 1945. The results of the investigation, published in book form under the title *The Death of Anton Webern: A Drama in Documents,*[1] included an account by Webern's eldest daughter, Mrs. Amalie Waller, who had been called upon to corroborate the findings. Several months later, Mrs. Waller communicated to the writer the existence of posthumous Webern manuscripts in the family's possession. The materials, mostly still unpublished, included a quantity of compositions, diaries, a stage play, and other writings.

During the early summer of 1961, arrangements were completed to acquire this entire estate for the Moldenhauer Archive, a research collection devoted to furthering the study of music history through primary sources. This extensive collection of

[1] New York: Philosophical Library, 1961.

original manuscripts, letters, and documents aims to provide a survey of all stylistic periods, but it is the twentieth century which is most systematically and comprehensively represented. The project was initiated during the early fifties and has been open to scholarship since its inception. While previous centuries are well documented with significant manuscripts by most of their leading musical exponents and a wealth of association items, special attention has been devoted to locating and preserving twentieth-century materials of potential importance which might otherwise have been lost to future study. After this primary function of the archivist, dissemination takes place through the channels of performance, study, and publication, and the creative process is thus completed.

A nucleus of Webern autographs, including the *Trakl Lieder*, Opus 14, in a formerly unknown version for voice and piano, had already existed in the archive before the initial contact with Mrs. Waller. This small core was dramatically enlarged by the arrival of the posthumous Webern papers in the United States. The event, noted by the *New York Times* (September 4, 1961), created much excitement in music circles. In order to give the unknown early compositions their first hearings, within the context of a large-scale presentation of the composer's music, the First International Webern Festival was held at the University of Washington from May 25 to May 28, 1962. The International Webern Society was organized at the same time.

Spurred by the vision of a special Webern Archive, as it had been conceived by then, concerted efforts were made during the months and years following to gather as much additional material as possible. The sources were many and included Webern's family members, friends and collaborators, former pupils and patrons. Several field trips furthered these systematic collecting activities. A visit to Hildegard Jone, the poetess, in October, 1962, only a few months before her death, resulted in the acquisition of the original terra-cotta bust of Anton von Webern by Josef Humplik which is pictured in the frontispiece of this volume, of Jone's well-known oil painting portraying Webern in his fateful last hour, and of several other art objects important to the iconography of the Webern circle.

The momentum of these endeavors brought about another notable acquisition. In December, 1963, four large sketchbooks were unearthed and incorporated into the archive. Together with Webern's last sketchbook, which had formed part of the estate transferred in 1961, these volumes, containing a total of 422 folio pages, constitute an unbroken chain of Webern's musical thought during the last twenty years of his life. They comprise his entire *oeuvre* from 1926 onward and include, besides every already published work from Opus 19 through Opus 31, several hitherto unknown projects.

As if by providence, still another discovery, made late in October, 1965, was to link the entire earlier period of Webern's creative life with that covered by the sketchbooks. The hunt for a second Webern sculpture by Humplik, known only through a photograph, led to a dark attic in an old house near Vienna where, entirely accidentally, remnants of Webern's library and other belongings were uncovered along with the portrait bust. Salvaged from Webern's former home in Maria Enzersdorf during the chaotic weeks at the end of World War II, these materials, completely disarranged in the process, had slumbered in their hideaway, all but forgotten, for a full twenty years (see *New York Times,* April 10, 1966). Among the relics were found many "missing links" in Webern documentation, beginning with his earliest attempts at composition in 1899 and extending over the entire period of his creative work up to 1925. Again, a number of formerly unknown compositions came to light. Regrettably, but unavoidably, the production deadline of the present volume allowed for only a few weeks' extension after the discovery had been made. The complete cataloguing of all newly found materials therefore became impossible, and in some details the desired scrutiny through time-consuming research had to remain wanting. Because of the special circumstances, apologies must be offered for any incompleteness or inaccuracy in the listing of these most recent additions to the archive.

Beyond assembling a self-contained collection of Weberniana, providing an all but complete documentation of the composer's life and work, the archive also aims to afford an extensive survey of basic and peripheral influences shaping the world of Anton von Webern, or emanating from it. Arnold Schoenberg, Webern's revered teacher and friend, is represented by manuscripts, documents, and numerous letters. Some of the last are addressed to both Berg and Webern and contain discussions of problems common to the three. Webern's confrère, Alban Berg, is in evidence with over two hundred and fifty primary source documents including compositions, many letters, and drafts of critical essays.

The archive's perspectives range beyond the Viennese triumvirate of Schoenberg, Berg, and Webern to sources of influence like Debussy or Mahler and to the pioneering stage of atonality and twelve-tone technique, as in the experiments of Josef Matthias Hauer. Likewise, extensive documentation penetrates and reflects the generation that worked simultaneously with Webern, regardless of the variance in idioms and techniques employed by individual composers; the philosophy of the project aspires to be all-encompassing. Autograph scores by such masters as Apostel, Bartók, Blacher, Fortner, Hába, Hindemith, Krenek, Pisk, Stravinsky, Varèse, Wellesz, and Zillig, to mention only a few, bear witness to the development of musical thought and syntax evolving during that fertile era. The younger generation of composers, recognizing Webern's aesthetic as its model and fountainhead, is represented by such exponents as Berio, Birger-Blomdahl, Boulez, Dallapiccola, Foss, Ginastera, Hartmann, Henze, Lutoslawski, Nono, Penderecki, Petrassi, Pousseur, Rochberg, Schuller, Stockhausen, de la Vega, and Xenakis, again to name only a few. Regarding the work of Anton von Webern as cornerstone in the edifice of their new music, many of these composers are probing the technical and spiritual dimensions of our own day, bringing to fruition the prophecies of one of the great innovators in the art of music. With Webern's significance firmly established, the archive created in his name can serve as a storehouse of information for biographical data and musical analyses. The purposes and aspirations of the Webern Archive are twofold, yet inseparable: to provide a research center for Webern studies and, as museum, to stand as a fitting memorial to Webern's spirit.

CATALOGUE OF THE WEBERN ARCHIVE

The following catalogue of the Webern Archive, which constitutes an integral section within the Moldenhauer Archive, is arranged as follows:

I. Music manuscripts
II. Stage play; diaries; miscellaneous writings and notes
III. Letters
IV. Documents
V. Photographs
VI. Webern's library
VII. Personal relics
VIII. Art objects
IX. Association and reference materials (selected)

The number of pages given indicates written pages only, the blank pages not being counted. Measurements give height before width. Annotations are necessarily sketchy. In addition to the catalogue listings, there are numerous items of interest, such as many original manuscripts, letters, and documents by Webern's circle of friends, colleagues, and other contemporaries. Beyond such primary source materials, the collection extends into a comprehensive Webern reference library, including books, essays, programs, newspaper articles, scores, recordings, and related materials.

I. MUSIC MANUSCRIPTS

Two Pieces, for violoncello and piano (1899). (1) Marked "Langsam." Full score. 3 pp., 33 x 25.5 cm. Also cello part. 1 p., 33 x 25.5 cm. (2) Marked "Langsam" and dated "Pregelhof, 17. Scheiding, 1899." Full score. 2 pp., 33 x 25.5 cm. Also cello part. 1 p., 33 x 25.5 cm.

The same. Another full score of (2). 2 pp., 33 x 25.5 cm. Also an incomplete fair copy of (2). 1 p., 33 x 25.5 cm.

Three Poems, for voice and piano (1899-1903). (1) "Vorfrühling" (Ferdinand Avenarius). (2) "Nachtgebet der Braut" (Richard Dehmel). (3) "Fromm" (Gustav Falke). Full scores. 6 pp., 34.5 x 26.5 cm.

The same. Complete set of drafts. "Vorfrühling" contains indications for an intended instrumentation. 6 pp., various folio sizes.

Vorfrühling II (Ferdinand Avenarius), for voice and piano. Draft of Webern's setting of the second poem in the cycle. 2 pp., 33 x 25.5 cm.

Two Songs after Poems by Ferdinand Avenarius, for voice and piano (1900-1). (1) "Wolkennacht." (2) "Wehmut." Full scores. 6 pp., 33 x 25.5 cm.

Hochsommernacht (Martin Greif), for vocal duet and piano. Full score. 1 p., 34.5 x 26.5 cm.

Three Songs after Poems by Ferdinand Avenarius, for voice and piano (1903-4). [No definite order is indicated; the order here given is that employed in programing for the First International Webern Festival.] (1) "Gefunden." (2) "Gebet." (3) "Freunde." Full scores. 8 pp., 34.5 x 26.5 cm.

The same. Complete set of drafts. 5 pp., 34.5 x 26.5 cm.

Eight Early Songs, for voice and piano (1901-4). [No definite order is indicated; the order here given is that employed in programing for the First International Webern Festival.] (1) "Tief von fern" (Richard Dehmel). (2) "Aufblick" (Richard Dehmel). (3) "Blumengruss" (Goethe). (4) "Bild der Liebe"

(Martin Greif). (5) "Sommerabend" (Wilhelm Weigand). (6) "Heiter" (Friedrich Nietzsche). (7) "Der Tod" (Matthias Claudius). (8) "Heimgang in der Frühe" (Detlev von Liliencron). Full scores. 16 pp., and 3 pp. of related sketches, 34.5 x 26.5 cm.

The same. Complete set of drafts. On verso of "Der Tod," sketches of a canon. Also miscellaneous other sketches. 14 pp., 34.5 x 26.5 cm.; 2 pp., 16.5 x 26.5 cm.

Siegfrieds Schwert, ballad for voice and large orchestra, on a poem by Ludwig Uhland (1903). Full score. 15 pp., 34.5 x 26.5 cm.

Liebeslied (Hans Böhm), for voice and piano (1904). Draft. 1 p., 34.5 x 26.5 cm.

Im Sommerwind, idyll for large orchestra (1904). Based on a poem by Bruno Wille. Full score. 36 pp., 34.5 x 26.5 cm.

The same. Complete draft in condensed score, dated August 5, 1904. 12 pp., 34.5 x 26.5 cm.

The same. Preliminary sketches, including first concept of the Coda section. 3 pp., 16.5 x 26 cm.

Langsamer Satz, for string quartet (1905). Full score. 9 pp., 34.5 x 26.5 cm.

The same. Complete set of parts (two violins, viola, and violoncello), in the composer's hand. 13 pp., 34.5 x 26.5 cm.

The same. Sketches. 14 pp., 34.5 x 26.5 cm.; 2 pp., 17 x 26.5 cm.

Quartet, for string quartet (1905). On the verso of the title page, a quotation from the writings of Jacob Böhme. Full score. 22 pp., 34.5 x 26.5 cm.

The same. Complete draft, dated Pregelhof, August 24, 1905. 21 pp., 34.5 x 26.5 cm. On a separate sheet, changes of the finale, dated Vordernberg, September 12, 1905. 2 pp., 34.5 x 26.5 cm.

The same. An earlier sketch of the D major section. 2 pp., 34 x 27 cm.

The same. Preliminary sketches, entitled "Form Entwurf für ein Streichquartett nach Segantinis Tryptichon: Werden—Sein—Vergehn" and dated July 13, 1905. The sketches contain thematic materials and an outline for development of each of the sections. 14 pp., 17.5 x 13.5 cm.

Quartet in A minor, for string quartet. Sketches in full score. 27 pp., 35 x 26.5 cm.

The same. Violin II and cello parts in the composer's hand. 18 pp., 35 x 26.5 cm.

Rondo für Streichquartett, for string quartet. Full score. 15 pp., 34.5 x 26.5 cm.

The same. Complete set of parts in the composer's hand. 27 pp., 34.5 x 26.5 cm.

The same. Sketches in full score. 11 pp., 34.5 x 26.5 cm.

Satz für Klavier, for piano solo (ca. 1905-6). Complete set of sketches. 11 pp., 34.5 x 26.5 cm.

Sonatensatz für Klavier, for piano solo (ca. 1906). This piece, the title of which was later changed to Rondo, is most likely the sonata movement mentioned in Webern's lectures *The Path to the New Music* (p. 48; German edition, p. 52). Draft and sketches. 15 pp., 34.5 x 26.5 cm.

Quintet, for string quartet and piano (1906). The manuscript contains a few suggestions in the hand of Arnold Schoenberg, under whom Webern was studying at the time. Full score. 34 pp., 34.5 x 26.5 cm.

The same. Sketches in full score. 71 pp., 34.5 x 26.5 cm.

The same. Set of parts for the strings, written by a copyist, containing additional directions in the composer's hand. 45 pp., 34.5 x 26.5 cm.

Five Songs after Poems by Richard Dehmel, for voice and piano (1906-8). (1) "Ideale Landschaft." (2) "Am Ufer." (3) "Himmelfahrt." (4) "Nächtliche Scheu." (5) "Helle Nacht." Full scores. 15 pp., 34.5 x 26.5 cm.

The same. Sketches for "Ideale Landschaft." 2 pp., 34.5 x 26.5 cm.

Alladine und Palomides (1908). Sketch for Webern's intended opera, after the play by Maurice Maeterlinck. The project is mentioned in Webern's letter to Ernst Diez, written from Ischl on July 17, 1908. Sketched out is the opening of Act I, including a short prelude and the beginning of Ablamore's monologue. 1 p., 34 x 26.5 cm.

Passacaglia, for orchestra, Opus 1 (1908). Final draft in full score. 37 pp., 34.5 x 26.5 cm.

The same. Sketches in condensed score. 22½ pp., 34.5 x 26.5 cm.

Entflieht auf leichten Kähnen, for mixed chorus a cappella, Opus 2 (1908). In this score, the composer gives the chorus the instrumental assistance of violin, viola, violoncello, harmonium, and pianoforte. Full score. 7 pp., 26.5 x 34.5 cm. On p. 8 there appear four measures of a melody line.

Fünf Lieder aus *Der siebente Ring* von Stefan George, for voice and piano, Opus 3 (1907-8). (1) "Dies ist ein Lied." (2) "Im Windesweben." (3) "An Bachesranft." (4) "Im Morgentaun." (5) "Kahl reckt der Baum." Originally listed by the composer as Opus 2, including seven songs, of which four are used in the present cycle. Set of full scores. 16 pp., 35 x 26.5 cm.

The same. Earlier versions of "Dies ist ein Lied" and "Im Windesweben." Full scores. 5 pp., 34.5 x 26.5 cm.

The same. "Im Morgentaun." Fragment of first three measures. 1 p., 34.5 x 26.5 cm.

The same. Fair copies of "Dies ist ein Lied," "Im Windesweben," and "Kahl reckt der Baum," in a copyist's hand. With titles and various annotations in the composer's autograph. Full scores. 9 pp., 34.5 x 26.5 cm.

Fünf Lieder nach Stefan George, for voice and piano, Opus 4 (1908-9). (1) "Eingang." (2) "Noch zwingt mich Treue." (3) "Ja Heil und Dank dir." (4) "So ich traurig bin." (5) "Ihr tratet zu dem Herde." Full scores. On closing page, a note in the composer's hand: "Neun Lieder, Op. 6, nach Gedichten von Stefan George komponiert von Anton von Webern," and indication of publication intentions. 14 pp., 34.5 x 26.5 cm.

The same. Fair copies of "Eingang" and "Noch zwingt mich Treue," in a copyist's hand. Each song contains additions and corrections in the composer's autograph. Full scores. 9 pp., 34.5 x 26.5 cm.

The same. Two separate title pages, one giving a listing of the seven songs intended to be included in Opus 4, the other stating five songs for the definitive version of 1920. 2 pp., 34.5 x 26 cm.

Four Songs after Poems by Stefan George, for voice and piano (1908-9). (1) "Erwachen aus dem tiefsten Traumesschosse." (2) "Kunfttag I." (3) "Trauer I." (4) "Das lockere Saatgefilde lechzet krank." The first song is from George's *Das Jahr der Seele,* the other three stem from *Der siebente Ring.* According to title listings accompanying Opera 3 and 4, all four songs originally were intended for these cycles. Set of full scores. 14 pp., 33.5 x 26.5 cm.

Fünf Sätze für Streichquartett, for string quartet, Opus 5 (1909). Full score. 20 pp., 34.5 x 26.5 cm.

The same. First movement, measures 1-6, in an earlier version. Full score. 1 p., 34 x 26.5 cm.

The same. Violin I part, fragment of eight measures from the first movement. 1 p., 32.5 x 25 cm.

The same. Brief sketch for first movement, contained on same page with sketches for Opus 7. See Opus 7.

Fünf Sätze für Streichorchester, arranged from Opus 5 for string orchestra (1929). First movement (incomplete) and fourth movement (complete) in full scores. 5 pp., 33.5 x 27 cm.

The same. Sketches for all five movements, marked by the composer as second draft. Full score. 16 pp., 34 x 27 cm.

The same. Contrabass part, sketch for first movement. 1 p., 34 x 27 cm.

Sechs Stücke für Orchester, for orchestra, Opus 6 (1910). Third movement, measures 1-4, in full score. 1 p., 34.5 x 26.5 cm.

The same, in the composer's arrangement for chamber orchestra. Instrumental parts, written in Webern's hand, for flute, oboe, clarinet, large drum and triangle, tamtam, bells, harmonium, pianoforte, violin I, violin II, and viola. 53 pp., various sizes.

Vier Stücke für Geige und Klavier, for violin and piano, Opus 7 (1910). Full score. Originally marked as Opus 6, No. 1, and bearing a note "Endgiltige Fassung Sommer 1914." 10 pp., 34 x 26.5 cm.

The same. Complete violin part in the composer's hand. 6 pp., 40 x 29 cm.

The same. The first six measures of Piece No. 1 in full score. 1 p., 35 x 27 cm.

The same. Brief sketches for Pieces Nos. 2 and 3 (marked here by Webern as Nos. 2, 3, and 4). The page also contains short notations for Opus 5, No. 1. 1 p., 11.5 x 26.5 cm.

Zwei Lieder nach Gedichten von Rainer Maria Rilke, for voice and eight instruments, Opus 8 (1910). (1) "Du, der ichs nicht sage." (2) "Du machst mich allein." Full score, originally marked by the composer as Opus 7, No. 1, and designated as "I. Fassung." 7 pp., 34.5 x 26.5 cm.

The same. Marked by the composer: "3. Fassung 1921 (Jänner 1925, neuerdings umgearbeitet; für Drucklegung 4. Fassung)." 8 pp., 26.5 x 34.5 cm.

The same. Sketches for "Du, der ichs nicht sage" included with the foregoing. 1 p., 17 x 27 cm.

The same. Voice-piano score of both songs. 2 pp., 34.5 x 27 cm.

Sechs Bagatellen für Streichquartett, for string quartet, Opus 9 (1913). Full score, originally marked "II. Streichquartett." Besides the Six Bagatelles in their final version, another piece for voice and string quartet is included with this score. It is marked No. 2, and based on a text beginning "Schmerz immer blick nach oben." 13 p., 35 x 27 cm.

The same. Sketch for Bagatelle No. 6. 1 p., 28 x 27 cm.

Fünf Stücke für Orchester, for orchestra, Opus 10 (1911-13). Piece No. 4, measures 1-4, in full score. On verso, sketches for a song, dated 1920. 2 pp., 18 x 27 cm.

The same. Piece No. 5. Miscellaneous sketches. 1 p., 22 x 32.5 cm.

Four Pïeces for Orchestra (ca. 1910-13). Numbered by Webern: III (Bewegt), IV (Sehr bewegte Viertel), V (Langsame Viertel), and VI (Langsam, sostenuto). Resemble Opus 10 in instrumentation and general style, except that IV employs a larger orchestral complement and seems more closely related to Opus 6. Full scores. 18 pp., 35 x 27 cm.

O sanftes Glühn der Berge, song with orchestral accompaniment (1913). The instrumentation of this song is identical to that of Opus 10; the manuscript was found together with that listed under Opus 10, No. 5. Condensed score. 2 pp., 35 x 25 cm.

The same. Two sets of sketches in condensed score. 14 pp., 12 x 26.5 cm.

Drei kleine Stücke für Violoncello und Klavier, for violoncello and piano, Opus 11 (1914). With dedication: "Meinem lieben Vater" dated "z. 27. V. 1914," and initialed "T." [Toni]. Full score. 6 pp., 35 x 27 cm.

Cello Sonata, for violoncello and piano (1914). Draft in full score. 4 pp., 17.5 x 25 cm.

Vier Lieder, for voice and piano, Opus 12 (1915-17). (1) "Der Tag ist vergangen." (2) "Die geheimnisvolle Flöte." (3) "Schien mir's, als ich sah die Sonne." (4) "Gleich und gleich." Full score. 12 pp., 35 x 26.5 cm.

The same. Sketches included with the foregoing. 2 pp., 17 x 27 cm.; 1 p., 34 x 26.5 cm.

The same. Complete sketches of all four songs. 14 pp., 17.5 x 27 cm.

Vier Lieder, for voice and orchestra, Opus 13 (1914-18). (1) "Wiese im Park." (2) "Die Einsame." (3) "In der Fremde." (4) "Ein Winterabend." Full score. 34 pp., various folio sizes.

The same. Voice-piano score (Klavierauszug). 17 pp., 34.5 x 26.5 cm.

The same. Piano reduction. 9 pp., various sizes.

The same. Complete sketches in condensed score. 17 pp., 17.5 x 26.5 cm.; 3 pp., 28.5 x 38 cm.

The same. Miscellaneous sketches for "Wiese im Park" and "In der Fremde." 10 pp., 17.5 x 26.5 cm.

Two Songs, for voice and orchestra (1914). (1) "Leise Düfte." (2) "Nun wird es wieder Lenz." The instrumentation of these songs is identical to that of Opus 13. Drafts in condensed score. 6 pp., 17.5 x 25 cm.

Sechs Lieder nach Gedichten von Georg Trakl, for voice, clarinet, bass clarinet, violin, and violoncello, Opus 14 (1917-21). (1) "Die Sonne." (2) "Abendland I." (3) "Abendland II." (4) "Abendland III." (5) "Nachts." (6) "Gesang einer gefangenen Amsel." Full score. 23 pp., 34.5 x 26.5 cm.

The same. Voice-piano score (Klavierauszug). 15 pp., 21 x 34.5 cm.

The same. Piano reduction (1923). 9 pp., various sizes. One leaf, containing close of "Abendland II" and beginning of "Abendland III," is missing.

The same. Complete sketches in condensed score. 25 pp., various quarto sizes.

The same. Miscellaneous sketches for "Gesang einer gefangenen Amsel." 7 pp., 17 x 26.5 cm.

The same. Incipit to "Abendland III," voice and clarinet parts only. On verso, sketch for a song with instrumental accompaniment. 2 pp., 24 x 26.5 cm.

Fünf geistliche Lieder, for soprano and instrumental ensemble, Opus 15 (1917-22). (1) "Das Kreuz." (2) "Morgenlied" (from *Des Knaben Wunderhorn*). (3) "In Gottes Namen aufstehn." (4) "Mein Weg geht jetzt vorüber." (5) "Fahr hin, o Seel'." With two title pages, one of which indicates that the work was submitted for the Berkshire Chamber Music Prize (dated February 8, 1924). Full score. 20 pp., 34.5 x 26.5 cm.

The same. Voice-piano score (Klavierauszug). 9 pp., 21.5 x 34.5 cm.

The same. Sketches in full score for all five songs. 18 pp., various quarto sizes.

The same. "Fahr hin, o Seel'," condensed score. 1 p., 26.5 x 34.5 cm.

The same. "Fahr hin o, Seel'." Presentation copy bearing the inscription: "Frau Hildegard Jone in Herzlichkeit von Ihrem A. Webern. Mödling, d. 25. VI. 1929." A small photograph of Webern is pasted on the margin. Full score. 2 pp., 28.5 x 38.5 cm.

O Mutter, Dank! So fühl' ich deine Hand, for voice with orchestral accompaniment (1919). Sketches in condensed score. 5 pp., 17.5 x 26.5 cm.

Fünf Canons, nach lateinischen Texten, for soprano, clarinet, and bass clarinet, Opus 16 (1923-24). (1) "Christus factus est." (2) "Dormi Jesu." (3) "Crux fidelis." (4) "Asperges me." (5) "Crucem tuam adoramus." Full score. 7 pp., 21 x 34.5 cm.

The same. Sketches for all canons except "Dormi Jesu," in full score. 24 pp., various sizes.

Drei Volkstexte, for voice, violin (viola), clarinet, and bass clarinet, Opus 17 (1924). (1) "Armer Sünder, du." (2) "Liebste Jungfrau." (3) "Heiland, unsre Missetaten." Brief sketch for "Liebste Jungfrau," in full score. 1 p., 34 x 27 cm.

Kinderstück, for piano solo (1924). 2 pp., 34 x 27 cm.

Drei Lieder, for voice, clarinet, and guitar, Opus 18 (1925). (1) "Schatzerl klein." (2) "Erlösung." (3) "Ave, Regina." Full score. 10 pp., 34 x 27 cm.

The same. Sketches for "Ave, Regina." On p. 4, sketches for another song. 4 pp., 17 x 26 cm.

Satz für Streichtrio, for violin, viola, and violoncello (1925). Marked "Ruhig fliessend." Full score. 4 pp., 34 x 27 cm.

The same. Incipit, containing measure 1, in full score. 1 p., 34 x 27 cm.

String Trio, for violin, viola, and violoncello (1925). Marked "Ruhig," and independent from the foregoing work. Sketches in full score. 4 pp., 17 x 26.5 cm.

The same. Another draft, with variants. 2 pp., 17.5 x 27 cm.

The same. "Reihen zum Streich-Trio." Row chart; preliminary studies exploring the possibilities of the tone row. 2 pp., 17 x 26.5 cm.

Zwei Lieder auf Texte aus Goethes *Chinesisch-Deutsche Jahres- und Tageszeiten,* for mixed chorus with accompaniment of celesta, guitar, violin, clarinet, and bass clarinet, Opus 19 (1926). (1) "Weiss wie Lilien." (2) "Ziehn die Schafe von der Wiese." Full score. 10 pp., 34 x 27 cm.

The same. Piano reduction (Klavierauszug), dated 1928. 4 pp., 34 x 27 cm.

Opera 19 through 31 are contained in Five Sketchbooks, comprising Webern's entire *oeuvre* from 1926 to 1945. Bound in cardboard covers. A total of 422 pp. (397 pp. bound, 27 x 33.5 cm.; 25 pp. in loose leaves, various sizes). The sketchbooks afford a close study of Webern's creative processes. Dates and general descriptions here given largely follow Webern's own designations.

(I) January, 1926–Summer, 1929. 95 pp. Two Songs, Opus 19: closing section of the first chorus "Weiss wie Lilien," and second chorus "Ziehn die Schafe von der Wiese" (January, 1926). Sketches for a chorus "Auf Bergen in der reinsten Höhe" (Fall, 1926). String Trio, Opus 20, including sketches for a projected third movement (Summer, 1927). Symphony, Opus 21, including sketches for an unfinished third movement (January–Summer, 1928). Quartet, Opus 22, including sketches for an abandoned third movement (Spring–Summer, 1929); this work was first conceived as a concerto for violin, piano, clarinet, French horn, and string orchestra (Fall, 1928). Continuation on inserted sheets (Christmas, 1929). Sketches for a String Quartet (Spring, 1929). Sketches for a Song after Goethe (March, 1929).

(II) Christmas, 1929–August, 1934. 80 pp. Quartet, Opus 22. Sketches for miscellaneous songs. Sketches for an orchestral overture. Three Songs, Opus 23. Concerto, Opus 24, first and second movements. Three Songs, Opus 25, No. 1.

(III) August, 1934–March, 1938. 91 pp. Concerto, Opus 24, third movement. Three Songs, Opus 25, Nos. 2 and 3 (1934). Das Augenlicht, Opus 26 (1935). Variations for Piano, Opus 27 (1936). String Quartet, Opus 28 (1937-38).

(IV) June, 1938–January, 1943. 116 pp. First Cantata, Opus 29 (July 1, 1938–November 26, 1939); this work was first conceived by Webern as "II. Symphonie," in five movements. Variations for Orchestra, Opus 30 (April 15–November 26, 1940). Second Cantata, Opus 31, sketches for the first, fourth, fifth, and sixth movements (May 7, 1941–January 21, 1943).

(V) March, 1943–1945. 40 pp. Webern's last sketchbook, carried by him to Mittersill in 1945. Second Cantata, Opus 31, second and third movements. Sketches to an apparently abandoned poem for the same cantata (the tone row being the same); the text underlying these sketches originates from Hildegard Jone's unpublished poem "Verwandlung der Chariten." Sketches for the projected Third Cantata, using words from the *Lumen* cycle of Hildegard Jone ("Das Sonnenlicht spricht: Aufgeht der Vorhang der Nacht. Durch Licht wird die Herrlichkeit sichtbar . . ."), and amalgamating the original sketches for a *Konzert* in three movements (designated as: 1. Sonate; 2. Adagio; 3. Rondo).

I. Kantate, Opus 29, on texts by Hildegard Jone, for soprano solo, mixed chorus, and orchestra (1938-39). (1) "Zündender Lichtblitz." (2) "Kleiner Flügel, Ahornsamen." (3) "Tönen die seligen Saiten Apolls." Voice-piano score (Klavierauszug), contained in a cardboard cover with autograph title inscription. 24 pp., 34.5 x 26.5 cm.

The same. Webern's autograph copy of the poems by Hildegard Jone used for the cantata. The texts are written on two sheets, 4° and 8°, and were included with the foregoing score.

The same. Presentation copy in the composer's hand of the middle section, "Kleiner Flügel, Ahornsamen," for soprano solo and orchestra, with the inscription: "Hildegard Jone von Ihrem Anton Webern." Full score. 14 pp., 34.5 x 26.5 cm.

II. Kantate, Opus 31, on texts by Hildegard Jone, for soprano and bass soli, mixed chorus, and orchestra (1941-43). Complete score in condensed form, in six sections: Section I. 12 pp., 19 x 26.5 cm.; Section II. 15 pp., 17 x 26.5 cm.; Section III. 11 pp., 13.5 x 32.5 cm.; Section IV. 5 pp., 13 x 32.5 cm.; Section V. 12 pp., 19.5 x 26.5 cm.; Section VI. 7 pp., 19 x 26.5 cm. Accompanying this manuscript is an autograph note by the author of the cantata's texts, Hildegard Jone: "Die grosse Kantate, die 2. Kantate. 1944. Freundseligkeit."

Arrangements of works by Franz Schubert and Hugo Wolf

Romanze aus *Rosamunde,* by Franz Schubert, arranged by Anton von Webern for voice with orchestral accompaniment: 2 flutes, 2 oboes, 2 clarinets, 2 bassoons, 2 French horns, violins I and II, viola, cello, and contrabass. Full score. 6 pp., 34 x 26 cm.

Ihr Bild, by Franz Schubert, arranged by Anton von Webern for voice with orchestral accompaniment: same instrumentation as in the foregoing. Full score. 4 pp., 34 x 26 cm.

Der Wegweiser from *Die Winterreise,* by Franz Schubert, arranged by Anton von Webern for voice with orchestral accompaniment: same instrumentation as in the foregoing. Full score. 7 pp., 34 x 26 cm.

Three Songs by Hugo Wolf and Franz Schubert, arranged by Anton von Webern for voice with orchestral accompaniment: same instrumentation as in the foregoing. (1) "Lebe wohl," by Hugo Wolf. (2) "Du bist die Ruh," by Franz Schubert. (3) "Thränenregen" from *Die schöne Müllerin,* by Franz Schubert. Full score. 13 pp., 34 x 26 cm. The opening of "Lebe wohl" is missing.

Der Knabe und das Immelein, by Hugo Wolf, arranged by Anton von Webern for voice with orchestral accompaniment: same instrumentation as in the foregoing. Full score. 4 pp., 34 x 26 cm. Incomplete.

Three Piano Sonatas by Franz Schubert, arranged by Anton von Webern for an orchestra of flutes, oboes, clarinets, bassoons, horns, and strings. (1) Sonata in A Minor, Opus 42. Second movement, measures 1-52. (2) Sonata in E-flat Major, Opus 122. Third movement, measures 1-36. (Minuet, without Trio.) (3) Sonata in B Major, Opus 147. Second movement, measures 1-13, and third movement, measures 1-53. Full scores. A total of 17 pp., 34 x 26 cm.

Denk es, o Seele! by Hugo Wolf, arranged by Anton von Webern for voice and large orchestra. Added to the instrumentation of the foregoing arrangements are 2 trumpets, 3 trombones, harp, and percussion. Dated Pregelhof, April 16, 1903. Full score. 10 pp., 35 x 26.5 cm.

Arrangements and copies of works by Arnold Schoenberg

Sechs Orchester-Lieder, Opus 8, by Arnold Schoenberg, arranged by Anton von Webern for voice and piano. No. II, "Das Wappenschild." Sketches, queries, and comments. 3 pp., 14.5 x 36.5 cm. No. VI, "Wenn Vöglein klagen." Piano reduction. 3 pp., 34.5 x 26.5 cm.

Kammersymphonie, Opus 9, by Arnold Schoenberg, arranged by Anton von Webern for flute (or second violin), clarinet in A (or viola), violin, violoncello, and piano. Webern's manuscript bears the dateline: "Beg. am 3. Nov. 1922." Full score. 60 pp., 21 x 34.5 cm.; 6 pp., various smaller sizes.

Friede auf Erden, Opus 13, by Arnold Schoenberg, for mixed chorus a cappella. Webern's manuscript, marked "1908 September," contains the vocal parts, without text, written on two systems. 6 pp., 34.5 x 26.5 cm.

The same. This score adds to the chorus a complement of assisting instruments: 2 flutes, 2 oboes, 2 clarinets, 2 bassoons, 2 horns, and strings. A prefatory note stipulates purpose and rendition of the orchestral accompaniment. The manuscript, in an autography still to be identified, bears Webern's markings and his signature of ownership on the title page. Found among Webern's posthumous papers, the score was obviously used by him in preparation of the 1928 performance. Full score. 36 pp., 34 x 27 cm.

Fünf Orchesterstücke, Opus 16, by Arnold Schoenberg, arranged by Anton von Webern for two pianos. (1) "Vorgefühle." (2) "Vergangenes." (3) "Sommermorgen an einem See" ("Farben"). (4) "Peripetie." (5) "Das obligate Rezitativ." In Webern's manuscript, the five movements are numbered, but untitled. Two-piano score. 26 pp., 34.5 x 27 cm.

Gurrelieder (1900-11), by Arnold Schoenberg. Vorspiel, arranged for two pianos, eight hands. Marked 1910; a performance of Webern's arrangement is recorded as early as January 14, 1910. Two-piano score. 13 pp., 34 x 26.5 cm.

Three Folksongs (Fifteenth and Sixteenth Centuries), arranged for four-part mixed chorus a cappella by Arnold Schoenberg. Fair copies in Webern's autograph. (1) "Es gingen zwei Gespielen gut" (folk tune, before 1540). Full score. 7 pp., 34 x 27 cm. (2) "Herzlieblich Lieb, durch Scheiden" (melody, fifteenth century). Full score. 3 pp., 34 x 27 cm. (3) "Schein uns, du liebe Sonne" (Antonius Scandellus, 1570). Full score. 3 pp., 33.5 x 27 cm. Webern copied the Schoenberg settings presumably in preparation for their first performance (Nos. 2 and 3 only) in November, 1929, by the Singverein under his direction.

Four German Folksongs (Fifteenth and Sixteenth Centuries), arranged for voice and piano by Arnold Schoenberg. (1) "Der Mai tritt ein mit Freuden" (folk tune, before 1545). 3 pp., 34.5 x 26.5 cm. (2) "Es gingen zwei Gespielen gut" (folk tune, before 1540). 3 pp., 34.5 x 26.5 cm. (3) "Mein Herz in steten Treuen" (composer unknown, fifteenth century). 3 pp., 34.5 x 26.5 cm. (4) "Mein Herz ist mir gemenget" (composer unknown, fifteenth century). 3 pp., 34.5 x 26.5 cm. This set of voice-piano scores, copied by Felix Greissle, was used by Webern, whose penciled marks of interpretation are found in each song.

Uncatalogued

As this volume went to press, several hundred pages of music manuscripts were still untabulated, ranging from student exercises and arrangements to works of the mature period (to ca. 1925), and comprising sketches, fragments, and finished scores. Media include solo, chamber ensemble, small and large orchestra. Only a general indication of these materials can be given here, in roughly chronological order. Where dates are indicated, these are as given by the composer.

Early songs with piano accompaniment.

Numerous compositions for piano solo.

Zum Schluss, song for voice and large orchestra, probably an arrangement.

Minuet and Trio in A minor for string quartet, marked "Lebhaft —die Betonungen zart."

Extensive work for large orchestra, in F major, marked "Kräftig bewegt."

Extensive composition for large orchestra, in D major, marked "Sehr bewegt."

Extensive piece for violin and piano.

Extensive composition for string orchestra, in D minor.

String Quartet in C, marked "Sehr bewegt." Possibly the quartet mentioned by Webern in his lectures, *The Path to the New Music* (p. 48; German edition, p. 52).

Two short movements in A minor for orchestra. One score, marked "Ruhig bewegt," is for large orchestra, the other for a smaller ensemble.

Miscellaneous drafts of instrumental compositions (1913-18).

Miscellaneous drafts of vocal compositions, with various instrumental accompaniments (1914-24). The texts employed in these compositions do not concur with those of any published songs.

Composition for wind and string instruments (1925).

German chorales, mostly in four-part harmonizations, including among others: "Christus, der ist mein Leben"; "Christ lag in Todesbanden"; "Nun freut euch, Gottes Kinder all' "; "O Ewigkeit, du Donnerwort"; "Herr Jesu Christ, dich zu uns wend' "; "Nicht so traurig, nicht so sehr"; "Gib dich zufrieden und sei stille"; "O Traurigkeit, o Herzeleid."

Included in the remaining bulk of manuscripts are miscellaneous harmony and counterpoint studies, copious materials scored for string quartet, and numerous orchestral sketches. It is probable that, with further scrutiny, some of the material from the uncatalogued group can be related to already known compositions.

II. STAGE PLAY; DIARIES; MISCELLANEOUS WRITINGS AND NOTES

Tot: Sechs Bilder für die Bühne (In memoriam . . . Oktober 1913). Stage play in six scenes, written in black ink (dialogue) and red ink (stage directions). Although couched in allegory, the play projects Webern's credo, a compound of very personal ideas and his submission to severe dogmatism. 35 pp., 23.5 x 15 cm., with stiff cover binding bearing the inscription: "Tot / Anton von Webern."

Eight Diaries and Notebooks. The numbers I through VI were assigned by Amalie Waller; the remaining two notebooks were added later.

(I) Records of concerts, operas, and plays, covering the period from 1900 to 1905. First journey to Bayreuth (1902), with musical quotations from *Parsifal* and *Meistersinger*. Impressions of Mahler, Strauss, Bruckner, Wolf, and other composers and conductors. Quotations and copies of poems. Notes about joint excursions with his future wife. Notebook. 104 pp., 19.5 x 12 cm.

(II) Extensive notes on operas by Richard Wagner and miscellaneous concerts. Original poems by Webern. Record of the first projected Opus 1, a cycle of five songs. (Date of origin of this notebook approximately concurrent with that of the first notebook.) 84 pp., 16 x 10 cm.

(III) Inscribed: "Meine Münchener Reise vom 20. Juli bis 6. September 1905." Detailed impressions of Webern's journey to Salzburg and Munich. Diary. 28 pp., 16.5 x 10 cm.

(IV) Notes on income during the years 1924-45. Detailed sources of revenue from publishers, patrons and private pupils. Notebook. 91 pp., 17 x 10.5 cm.

(V) Outlines of concert programs given, or planned to be given, by the Verein für musikalische Privataufführungen in Vienna, with listings of composers and works (1918–19). On p. 38, a statement of policy governing the performance of works, and their repetitions, signed by both Webern and Schoenberg and dated at Mödling, September 3, 1919. Notebook. 53 pp., 17 x 11 cm.

(VI) Webern's private diary (1916-39). Contains notes of a personal nature, mostly concerning family matters and professional high points. The diary closes with an entry, dated September 15, 1945, appended by Webern's widow, recording the deaths of "Toni" and their son Peter. Diary. 102 pp., 10.5 x 7.5 cm., with gold leaf, and bound in leather and brocade.

(VII) Outlines for concert programs of contemporary music, listing composers, selections, and performers. A supplement (ca. 1921) to item V above. Notebook. 23 pp., 20 x 16.5 cm.

(VIII) Quotations from works by Hölderlin (*Hyperion*), Thomas Mann, Rilke, and other authors. Catalogue of Webern's own *oeuvre* (Opera 1-31). Contained in this notebook are also copies, in Wilhelmine von Webern's hand, of Hildegard Jone's texts to Opera 23, 25, 26, 29, and 31. Notebook. 21 pp. (7 pp. in Anton von Webern's hand; 14 pp. in Wilhelmine von Webern's hand), 21 x 15 cm. Included with this volume, as loose leaves, were copies in Hildegard Jone's autograph of her cycles *Lumen* and *Enthüllte Form*.

A volume inscribed: "Bücher und Noten." An alphabetical catalogue of Webern's personal library, in his own hand. Literature and music are listed in separate sections. Dated June, 1914, with supplements of April, 1917, and May, 1918, and later entries up to 1929. 129 pp., in hard-cover binding, 16.5 x 10.5 cm.

Fair copy, in Webern's autograph, of all poems by Hildegard Jone set to music by him. Presumably written out in tribute to the poetess and preserved by the latter in a brocade cover. Included are "Drei Gesänge, Opus 23, aus *Viae inviae*"; "Drei Lieder, Opus 25"; "Das Augenlicht, Opus 26"; "I. Kantate, Opus 29"; and "II. Kantate, Opus 31." 12 pp., 20 x 14.5 cm.

Draft of an autobiographical sketch. 2 pp., 29 x 22.5 cm.

Draft of a *curriculum vitae*, including list of works up to Opus 11. 1 p., 17 x 10.5 cm.

List of early (pre-Opus 1) compositions. Contains songs, chamber and orchestral works. 2 pp., 20.5 x 15 cm.

List of all compositions from Opus 1 through Opus 22, including transcriptions. Year and locality of origin are given for each work. 1 p., 22.5 x 14 cm.

Literary concept for a musical composition based on ideas and characters occurring in the stage play *Tot.* 1 p., 20.5 x 15 cm.

Outline of seven different instrumental combinations to be employed in an orchestral work, presumably Opus 6 or Opus 10. With example in musical notation. 1 p., 17.5 x 27 cm.

Notes of corrections pertaining to vocal compositions, with examples of suggested changes. 2 pp., 10 x 10 cm.; 1 p., 16.5 x 9.5 cm. (This and the following two items were found between pages of Strindberg's *Blaubuch.*)

The text "Fahr hin, o Seel'," used for the double canon, Opus 15, No. 5, in Webern's autograph. With a note: "P. R. Erdsesen, 13. VI. 17, Kl." [1917, Klagenfurt] 1 p., 15 x 10 cm.

Two votive pictures, used by Webern as bookmarkers. One picture (Jesus blessing the people) bears on verso the composer's autograph inscription "Vater." Webern's writing on the other votive picture is undeciphered.

Notes on projects and programs, featuring works by Webern and other composers, and concerts to be conducted by him. 11 pp., in memorandum form, various sizes.

Draft of Webern's own program notes to Schubert's *Mass No. 6* in E-flat major, for a performance during the festival concert of the Mödlinger Männer-Gesang-Verein. 2 pp., 19.5 x 13.5 cm.

Dinner menu on the occasion of Arnold Schoenberg's fiftieth birthday. With humorous autograph comments and signatures by Arnold Schoenberg, Alban Berg, Anton von Webern, David Josef Bach, Paul Stefan, Marya Freund, and Marta Frank-Pisk (Vienna, September 13, 1924).

Autograph note by Adolf Loos, with Webern's authentication (February, 1933). 1 p., 10.5 x 15.5 cm.

"Kral. Vinohrady." Picture postcard with Webern's inscription on verso stating the extent of his stay in Prague ("12. VIII. 1917-31. V. 1918"), when he was theater conductor at the Deutsches Landestheater.

Picture postcard of a roadside shrine (*Marterl*), with inscription on verso commemorating the day of Webern's move from Mödling to Vienna (January 5, 1932).

Diary of a summer journey from Zell am See to Klagenfurt, including mountain climbs (August 20-28, 1931). 8 pp.: 4 pp., 21 x 17 cm.; 2 pp., 16.5 x 13.5 cm.; 2 typed pp. with autograph annotations, 20 x 16.5 cm.

"Partie ins Ötztal, 1934." Day-by-day account of a mountain excursion (August 12-22, 1934). 2 pp., 21.5 x 13.5 cm.

List of provisions and gear to be taken on an excursion, and two train timetables. 6 pp., on scrap paper, various sizes.

Fifteen envelopes containing inscribed picture postcards and other memorabilia from excursions and mountain climbs during the years 1923-37. This assembly represents Webern's own cherished collection of souvenirs. (For various postcard greetings mailed to family members from these excursions, see Section III). The inscribed envelopes are here counted as pages.

1. "Partie auf die Bürgeralm" (July 23-30, 1923). Diary notes and pressed flowers. 2 pp.

2. "Hochschwabpartie" (July 29, 1924). Diary notes. 11 pp.

3. "Schneealpe" (July 28, 1926). Hochschwab and other trips during 1926. Diary notes and pressed flowers. 5 pp.

4. "Partie Schneealpe" (July 11-12, 1928). Diary notes. 3 pp.

5. "Aufenthalt St. Wolfgang" (July 16-22, 1928). Diary notes. 2 pp.

6. "Reise nach Klagenfurt" (July 26–August 2, 1928). Diary notes and pressed flowers, including edelweiss and flowers from the graves of Webern's parents in Klagenfurt and Schwabegg. 4 pp.

7. "Sommer 1929. Vordernberg." Diary notes and pressed flowers. 5 pp.

8. "Dachstein" (Summer, 1930). Diary notes with pressed flowers and photographs taken by Webern's friend Ludwig Zenk. 4 pp.

9. "Sommer 1931. Vordernberg." Diary notes and pressed flowers received from Webern's daughters Amalie and Maria. 4 pp.

10. "Tour ins Glocknergebiet" (July 19-28, 1931). Diary notes. 20 pp.

11. "Vöslau-Gainsarn u. Bad Fusch" (Summer, 1932). Diary notes and three snapshots showing Webern at Zell am See and Bad Fusch. 14 pp.

12. "Sommer 1933. Jochberg. Kitzbühel." Diary notes and pressed alpine flowers. 4 pp.

13. "Sommer 1934. Ötztal." Diary notes. 4 pp.

14. "Sommer 1935. Venediger." Diary notes. 3 pp.

15. "Utendorf, Bichlwirt" (July 27–August 8, 1936) and "Ötztal" (July, 1937). Diary notes and pressed flowers, gathered on a climb of the Brustkogel. 8 pp.

III. LETTERS

Letters written by Webern

Four letters to Wilhelmine Mörtl, his future wife, to addresses in Geneva and Paris. Vienna, June 11/12, 1906. Vienna, June 22, 1906. Berlin, October 30, 1910. Berlin, November 29/30, 1910. 21 pp., 4° and 8°, with three addressed envelopes.

Christmas letter to his sister Rosa, extolling Vienna as the home of the greatest artists such as Beethoven and Schubert, and recalling the times the family spent there. Danzig, December 21, 1910. 4 pp., 12°.

Five letters and five postcards to his sister Rosa and her husband Otto Warto (1924-45). The correspondence treats mostly of family matters and includes a detailed account of the death of Peter von Webern (letter dated March 8, 1945). One postcard is written from Barcelona (April 9, 1932). The letter of Christmas, 1939, is written on the verso of a photograph of Webern. 16 pp., various sizes, with two addressed envelopes.

Five postcards to family members sent by Webern from various excursions: (1) To his daughter Amalie (Mürzzuschlag, July 28, 1926). (2) To his daughter Christine (St. Wolfgang, July 18, 1928). (3) To his son Peter (St. Wolfgang, July 20, 1928). (4) To their son Peter, written by Wilhelmine and cosigned by Anton von Webern (Zell am See, August 20, 1931). (5) To his wife Wilhelmine (Sölden, August 15, 1934).

Three letters and one postcard to his daughter-in-law Hermine, all dated 1945. The first (March 30) is written on the eve of Anton and Wilhelmine von Webern's flight from Maria Enzersdorf to Mittersill. The second, a postcard (early July), is a ten-word message sent through Red Cross emergency services (it reached the addressee only on October 16). The letter from Mittersill (June 13/July 13) and the last letter from Zell am See (August 30) describe conditions at the family's mountain refuge and inquire about belongings left behind, including music manuscripts. 13 pp., various sizes, with three addressed envelopes. Included is a letter by Wilhelmine von Webern (August 31). 3 pp., 8°.

Nine letters and four postcards to his cousin Ernst Diez, containing extensive discussions of musical experiences and aspirations, university studies, and other topics. One postcard is cosigned by Webern's father. (Klagenfurt and Vienna, 1900-34). 55 pp., 8°, with six addressed envelopes.

Draft of a petition to a high official, requesting that Arnold Schoenberg be exempted from military service during World War I. 2 pp., 16°.

Seven letters and forty-eight postcards to Josef Polnauer, on musical and personal matters. One letter is written by Webern's daughter Christine, with postscripts by Anton and Wilhelmine von Webern. (1914-41.) 103 pp., various sizes, with four addressed envelopes.

Five letters to Dr. Norbert Schwarzmann, mostly on private topics (1926-31). Two letters bear the postscripts of Webern's young daughter Christine. 9 pp., 8°, with three addressed envelopes.

Six letters to Ruzena Herlinger, on personal and musical matters (1926-36). 8 pp., autograph, 4° and 8°; 1 p. typed, 4°; with four addressed envelopes.

Seven letters to Adolph Weiss, on important musical projects and personal plans (1930-34). 12 pp. autograph, 8°; 4 pp. typed, 4° and 8°.

Three letters to Mrs. Emil Hertzka, the wife of Webern's publisher. Maria Enzersdorf: November 24, 1933; May 5, 1934; July 12, 1934. 5 pp., 8°.

Letter to Julius Schloss, referring to conditions in Vienna, Alban Berg's progress on *Lulu,* and Schoenberg's move to Boston (Vienna, December 29, 1933). 1 p., 8°, with addressed envelope. Also a postcard to Schloss, written by Hans Erich Apostel on the eve of Webern's fiftieth birthday and cosigned by Webern, Krenek, Steuermann, and Reich. (Vienna, December 2, 1933.)

Letter to Paul Amadeus Pisk, regarding Pisk's resignation as secretary of the Austrian Section of the I.S.C.M. Maria Enzersdorf, May 7, 1934. 1 p., 8°.

Six letters and twenty-nine postcards to Johann Humpelstetter. The correspondence (1934-45) begins with the disbandment of the Singverein, of which Humpelstetter was a member, and continues through the years of World War II. 65 pp. autograph, 3 pp. typed, various sizes, with four addressed envelopes. Also copy of a letter from Webern to Humpelstetter, dated December 14, 1943, which the addressee destroyed in line with military orders before being taken prisoner of war.

Letter to Alban Berg, acknowledging receipt and dedication of Berg's "Lied der Lulu," and describing the deep impression which this music makes upon him. December 25, 1934. 1 p., 8°.

Eight letters and three postcards to the Swiss painter Franz Rederer, mainly concerning private matters, but also discussing Webern's musical activities such as his instrumentation of

J. S. Bach's *Ricercar* (1934-39). 13 pp. autograph, 5 pp. typed, various sizes.

Eighteen letters to Willi Reich, dealing extensively with musical matters (1938-44). 28 pp., typed (single spaced), 4°, with numerous autograph additions. (These letters are published in part in *Anton Webern: Der Weg zur neuen Musik*, edited by Willi Reich.)

Four letters and five postcards to Karl Amadeus Hartmann, on professional and personal topics (1941-44). 7 pp. autograph, 2 pp. typed, various sizes.

For facsimile reproductions and typed copies of letters written by Webern, see Section IX.

Letters to and about Webern

Two letters and one postcard to Webern from his father Carl, commenting on the son's difficulties in securing an adequate position, and making caustic reference to Arnold Schoenberg (Pregelhof, 1910; Klagenfurt, 1918). 7 pp., various sizes.

Two official letters by the Mayor of Vienna, informing Webern of the award of the "Preis der Stadt Wien für Musik" for the years 1924 and 1931. An autograph notation by Webern, on the first of these two letters, denotes that the 1924 prize carried 1,000 schillings in award money, and that of 1931, 3,000 schillings (Vienna, June 24, 1924; Vienna, April 29, 1931). 2 pp., 4°.

Two letters to Webern by his cousin Ernst Diez, written from the United States (Bryn Mawr, Pa., 1936 and 1939). Both letters show underscorings in Webern's hand, and the first letter bears his autograph note "Schubert-Tänze," with reference to radio performances of which his correspondent has informed him. 6 pp., 8°.

Eleven letters to Webern by Erwin Stein, concerned with the publication, by Boosey and Hawkes, of Webern's *Quartet*, Opus

28. Also three letters by C. A. Rosen, two letters by Alfred Kalmus, and one letter by Ralph Hawkes (London, 1938-39). 25 pp., various sizes. Ten letters bear notes in Webern's hand.

Letters by Arnold Schoenberg to Webern and Berg: see Introduction.

Forty communications by Wilhelmine von Webern to Josef Humplik and Hildegard Jone (twenty-eight letters, six postcards), Ernst and Beryl Diez (three letters), Johann Humpelstetter (two letters), and Josef Polnauer (one letter). The correspondence encompasses the years 1936-49 and contains many poignant observations, such as the neglect of Webern's music after his death. 95 pp., various sizes, with seven addressed envelopes.

Extensive file of correspondence related to Webern study. The writers include Webern's sister Rosa, his daughter Amalie, his son Peter, and other family members; the poetess Hildegard Jone; colleagues, students, and friends.

Letter by Universal Edition to the Austrian Department of the Interior, Vienna, stressing the importance of Webern's posthumous manuscripts and urging their immediate transfer from Mittersill to Vienna. The official request seeks travel permission for Leopoldine Gross and Hermine von Webern, as the firm's trustees for this assignment, to cross the border between the Russian-held and American-occupied zones. The letter bears an affidavit of the Department of Education and Culture, attesting to the urgency of the mission. (Permission was ultimately denied.) Vienna, October 16, 1945. 1 p., 4°.

Two letters by Ludwig Zenk to Ernst Diez, containing a full account of Webern's death and reports on Webern's family and the dismal conditions in Vienna (December 10, 1946; February 4, 1947). 12 pp., 8°.

Letter by Werner Riemerschmid to Josef Polnauer, describing in detail the conditions at Webern's abandoned home in Maria

Enzersdorf during December 1945, and his own part in salvaging portions of the composer's papers (Mödling, March 9, 1947). 1 p., 4°, with addressed envelope.

IV. DOCUMENTS

Genealogy of the von Webern family. Established ca. 1939 by Anton von Webern for the purpose of proving Aryan descent, as then requested by the Hitler regime.

1. Complete listing of the family lineage in Webern's autograph. 2 pp., 34 x 21 cm.

2. Full documentation of the family ancestry. The file of forty-five original documents and notarized copies begins with the baptismal certificate (1778) of the composer's great-grandfather, Josef Eduard von Webern, and extends over five generations to Peter von Webern, the composer's son and last male member of the line. The file comprises all essential documents both of Webern's ancestry and that of his wife. (Included also are birth, marriage, and death certificates of Anton and Wilhelmine von Webern.) Twenty-eight documents bear descriptive annotations in Webern's autograph, and three paper folders labeled in his hand classify the records.

Four formal announcements of betrothal. (1) Wedding of the composer's parents, Carl von Webern to Amalie, née Geer. Leoben, October 8, 1877. (2) Engagement of the composer's aunt Marie von Webern to Friedrich Diez. Prävali, January, 1877. (3) Wedding of the composer's uncle Anton Weber von Webern to Marie, née Edle von Luschin. Laibach-Vienna, August, 1893. (4) Wedding of the composer's eldest daughter Amalie von Webern to Gunther Waller. Vienna, August, 1935.

Honorary doctorate conferred upon Carl von Webern by the Montanistische Hochschule at Leoben. Issued July 8, 1907, the diploma cites the recipient's merits in the field of mining science.

Printed calling card of Dr. Mont. h. c. Carl von Webern, K. K. Sektionschef I. R., Klagenfurt, with Anton von Webern's autograph annotations of date and street address.

Webern's graduation certificate, including record of grades, issued by the Gymnasium at Klagenfurt, July 11, 1902.

Replica of Webern's doctoral diploma, duplicated by the University of Vienna for the occasion of the Anton von Webern Memorial Exhibition in Seattle (1962) to replace the original document destroyed as a result of World War II. The reproduction, in imperial folio format, bears the university seal and the signatures of its 1962 officials.

Webern's last passport, with photo and signature. Issued at Vienna, January 10, 1940, and containing special visas for trips abroad. The last journey to Winterthur is recorded, under auspices of Dr. Werner Reinhart.

Last identity card, issued by the Mittersill police on September 13, 1945, and giving personal data (weight: 50 kg.). Signed twice by Webern. This identification card was carried by him at the time of his death, and the hole in the document presumably resulted from a bullet.

Invitation to attend a memorial ceremony for Hugo Wolf on March 29, 1903, for the purpose of raising funds for his grave. Printed on black-bordered stationery. Webern preserved this invitation in his library, inserted between the pages of Wagner's *Tannhäuser* score.

Certificate of membership in the Dürer Bund. Issued at Munich, August 4, 1903, for Anton von Webern, stud. phil., then residing at Pregelhof.

Two formal calling cards, one with imprint "Anton von Webern," the other "Dr. Anton Webern," and giving address at Maria Enzersdorf.

Festschrift Arnold Schoenberg zum 60. Geburtstag. No. 3 of the fifty copies issued. Numbered and assigned to Hildegard Jone in Webern's hand.

The same. No. 34 of this limited edition. Numbered and assigned to Ruzena Herlinger in Webern's hand.

Anton Webern prospectus issued by Universal Edition, containing information and picture. With Webern's autograph corrections and additions.

"Ein Brief Arnold Schönbergs." Polemic newspaper article, January 23, 1916, bearing a note in Webern's hand and kept in his library.

File of printed newsletters and programs of the Verein für musikalische Privataufführungen in Wien (1919-20). Issue No. 12 contains a survey of programs 1-100, listing composers, works, and performers. This brochure and others contain Webern's autograph annotations. Fifteen pieces, including some duplicates.

Large display poster of the Verein für musikalische Privataufführungen, Leitung Arnold Schönberg, for its "4 Propaganda Abende" (1919). Contains full programs and list of performers, including Webern. The poster, as well as the foregoing file of newsletters and programs, was found among Webern's papers.

Seven festival and concert programs, and three related newspaper articles (1920-38). Also found in Webern's library and bearing various notes in his hand. Festivals included are the Mahler Festival at Amsterdam (1920); the XIII. Festival of the International Society for Contemporary Music at Prague (1935); the XVI. Festival of the same organization at London (1938). At Prague the world première of Webern's *Konzert*, Opus 24, took place, and at London that of *Das Augenlicht*, Opus 26. The other programs list performances of Webern's *Vier Lieder*, Opus 13, and of his orchestral arrangement of Schubert's *Deutsche Tänze* by the Musikkollegium Winterthur under H. Scherchen, the Pullman Orchestra of Vienna, and via radio broadcast.

Certificate of testimony from the Mödlinger Männer-Gesang-Verein. Given to its conductor, Anton von Webern, after a performance of Bruckner's *F-minor Mass*. Signed by the chorus members and dated at Mödling, May 10, 1925.

Membership card (1934/35) for Johann Humpelstetter in the Verein für neue Musik, Sektion Österreich der internationalen Gesellschaft für neue Musik, with Anton von Webern's signature as the society's president.

Three receipts for money orders sent by Universal Edition and Stagma. The verso of one receipt contains Webern's own accounting.

Death announcement of Peter von Webern, the composer's only son. Two proofs of the printed announcement, which was set in type by the monks of St. Gabriel Abbey under Anton and Hermine von Webern's personal supervision. On a slip of paper, Webern's autograph stipulations for dimensions. Also a finished copy of the death announcement, issued by the widow, parents, and sisters (Perchtoldsdorf / Maria Enzersdorf, March 3, 1945).

Train ticket from Neulengbach to Mittersill. This is the ticket used for Webern's last flight from Vienna. Issued March 31, 1945.

Notification to Wilhelmine von Webern at Mittersill from the Finanzamt Mödling, granting her petition for income-tax exemption. Dated November 22, 1945.

Official disposition concerning the estate of Anton von Webern, naming his widow as beneficiary. Assets of the estate are stipulated at Sch. 1,168. Resolved by the District Court at Mödling, May 26, 1948.

Printed death announcement of Wilhelmine von Webern, issued by all members of the immediate family. Mittersill / Vienna, December 31, 1949. Three copies. One of the announcements is contained in an envelope addressed to Hildegard Jone, with a photograph of Wilhelmine von Webern included. Another announcement is addressed to Josef Polnauer.

Official disposition concerning the estate of Wilhelmine von

Webern, with names of the heirs, as resolved by the District Court of Mittersill, June 13, 1950.

Sechs Stücke für grosses Orchester, Opus 4. Appearing in facsimile reproduction under Webern's own imprint ("Im Selbstverlag des Komponisten"), this work was later published as Opus 6. In this earlier version, differences exist in instrumentation, scoring, and tempo indications. The title page bears Webern's autograph inscription: "Meinem lieben Vater, Klagenfurt, April, 1913."

"No. 3 aus Vier Stücke für Streichquartett." Later published as No. 4 of *Sechs Bagatellen,* Opus 9. Facsimile reproduction of the manuscript score, given by Webern to his father and, after the latter's death, preserved by Rosa Warto, as was the foregoing item.

"Der Tag ist vergangen." No. 1 of *Vier Lieder,* Opus 12. Printed as insert for *Musikblätter des Anbruch,* May, 1922, issue. This copy contains numerous corrections and additions in the composer's hand.

Printed copies with Webern's autograph dedications to Josef Humplik and/or Hildegard Jone. (1) *Passacaglia,* Opus 1. Full score, copy No. 80 of the first edition. Inscribed on title page: "Hildegard Jone und Josef Humplik mit den herzlichsten Weihnachtsgrüssen 1930 von Ihrem Webern." (2) *Sechs Bagatellen,* Opus 9. Inscribed on title page: "Sehr verehrte Frau Jone, ich weiss gar nicht, ob Sie Noten lesen können; aber wenn nicht: vielleicht verrät Ihnen das 'Bild,' das *diese* ergeben im Verein mit den ihnen von Schönberg vorangeschickten Worten etwas von dem, was sie enthalten. Das würde sehr freuen Ihren Ihnen sehr ergebenen. A. Webern. Mödling, Sommer 1927." A portrait photograph of Webern, with his autograph signature, is glued in as frontispiece. (3) *Zwei Lieder,* Opus 19. Inscribed on title page: "Liebe Freunde, wieder einmal *Noten-Bilder!* Sollten sie ein wenig 'Anklang' finden wäre sehr glücklich Ihr Anton Webern. Weihnachten 1928." (4) *Drei Gesänge aus Viae inviae,* Opus 23. Inscribed on title page: "Was Dir gehört, so wie mir, liebe Hildegard, nimm es entgegen mit Humplik von Deinem Anton Webern. Mai, 1936." Below the composer's dedication is an inscription in the autograph of the poetess: "Alle die Künste sind wahrlich Geschwister: Form, Klang, Vers u. Farbwelt. Sucht sie zur Einheit im Sein! Hildegard Jone-Humplik." (5) *Das Augenlicht,* Opus 26. Voice-piano score by Ludwig Zenk. Inscribed on title page: "'. . . und strömt als Freude sanft zurück' . . . Dir, liebe Hildegard, und Humplik, von Eurem Webern. Mai 1938."

Printed copy of *Trio,* Opus 20, with Webern's autograph inscription to Ernst Diez on title page: "S. l. Ernst, Mödling, Weihnachten 1927. A. W."

Another printed copy of *Trio,* Opus 20, with autograph dedication: "Frau Ruzena Herlinger in herzlichster Verehrung, Weihnachten, 1927, Anton Webern."

Alban Berg's concert aria *Der Wein.* Ruzena Herlinger's personal copy (first printed edition) with Webern's penciled directions for interpretation, made during coaching sessions. Also some annotations by the composer and, in red ink, the Czech version of the text in Mme Herlinger's hand.

V. PHOTOGRAPHS

Two formal portrait photographs of Anton von Webern, each with his autograph signature (1912 and 1935).

Two portrait photographs of Anton von Webern, bearing autograph inscriptions to his younger sister Rosa. (1) Taken at Prague in December, 1922, and dated "Mödling, Februar 1923." (2) Marked "April 1926, VIII. Symphonie von Mahler."

Portrait photograph, with Webern's autograph signature, given to his son Peter.

Photograph of Anton von Webern. On verso, the composer's autograph quotation from the second song of *Drei Gesänge aus*

Viae inviae, Opus 23, vocal part, with text, first six measures. Dedicated to Franz Rederer and dated June, 1936.

Photograph of Wilhelmine von Webern with first-born daughter Amalie. Dated by A. v. Webern "1914" at Stettin.

Three group photographs of Webern, Schoenberg, and Stein at Holland's North Sea coast. One of the photographs dated "1914" by Webern.

Four photographs of Webern's study at Neusiedlerstrasse 58 in Mödling. The year "1931" is inscribed by Webern on the verso of each photograph.

Seven photographs from the family album, showing Webern working in his garden, his daughter Maria, several grandchildren, and the house in Mödling. Two of the photographs bear Webern's notes.

Three formal portrait photographs of Anton von Webern in early childhood. Pictured also are sisters and parents.

Snapshot of Webern in military uniform, holding his daughter Amalie by the hand (1916).

Group photograph of the Singverein, including its conductor Webern, taken at an outing to the Höllenstein on May 28, 1927.

Three Webern photographs from the library of Julius Schloss, including two portraits and a photograph showing Webern rehearsing Mahler's *Sixth Symphony.*

Webern in the high Alps. Two photographs by Ludwig Zenk, one with the photographer's description on verso.

Thirty-five negatives of photographs picturing Webern at various periods of his life, his family, and friends. Many of these photographs are unpublished. Also prints and enlargements thereof.

Large portrait photograph of Anton von Webern, with inscription by his daughter Amalie.

Large group portrait of the Webern family, assembled before the Pregelhof on May 17, 1887. Shown are family members from grandfather Anton to the youngest generation, including the future composer, his sisters, and cousins. Also a photograph of the Pregelhof estate's manor house.

Family album of cabinet photographs, assembled by Marie von Webern, the composer's aunt. Contains ninety-two portraits, beginning with Anton von Webern's paternal grandparents.

Formal portrait photograph of Carl von Webern, with autograph dedication to his sister Marie (1882).

Two portrait photographs of Peter von Webern (1943 and 1944), and two photographs of his grave at Maribor, Yugoslavia, taken in 1954 by his widow Hermine.

VI. WEBERN'S LIBRARY

Items in the following list, although coming to the Webern Archive from various sources, at one time all belonged to the composer's personal library. See also Webern's own library catalogue, "Bücher und Noten," listed in Section II.

Music

Eduard Brunner. "Compositionen von Eduard Brunner für Amalie Geer, 1866." A volume of pianoforte compositions by the music teacher of Webern's mother, in Brunner's autograph. Included are a sonata, a fantasy, and numerous genre pieces. Webern preserved this volume among his own manuscripts.

Gustav Mahler. "Lob der Kritik," for voice and piano. This music manuscript, in Mahler's hand, was one of Webern's treasured possessions. 3 pp., 32 x 25 cm. Also a picture of Gustav Mahler.

Robert Schumann. "Ouverture zu Goethes Hermann und Dorothea für Orchester, Opus 136." Manuscript of the full score, by an unidentified copyist, with penciled markings in Webern's hand.

Franz Liszt. "Arbeiterchor," in Webern's transcription for bass solo, mixed chorus, and orchestra. Facsimile of the voice-piano score, with markings in Webern's hand.

Anton von Webern. "II. Kantate," Opus 31. Facsimile reproduction of the composer's autograph of the full score.

Arnold Schoenberg. *Verklärte Nacht,* Sextet, Opus 4. With Webern's autograph note "April 1906."

Arnold Schoenberg. *Sechs Orchester-Lieder,* Opus 8, No. 1, voice-piano score by Anton von Webern. With a note in Webern's hand on cover.

Arnold Schoenberg. *Gurre-Lieder.* First edition of the full score, with Webern's signature of ownership.

Arnold Schoenberg. *Die glückliche Hand,* Opus 18. With Webern's autograph note: "Uraufführung: 14. Oktober 1924. Wien. Volksoper." Schoenberg's autograph inscription to Webern reads: "Lieber Webern, Ich ahnte nicht, dass ich Dir die 'Glückliche Hand' noch nicht gereicht habe. Könnte doch wenigstens eine glückliche Hand von mir (wenigstens dem, der sie begreift) Glück bringen. Aber leider: Glück, ja; an der Fingerspitze! Mehr nicht! Aber mir scheint, Du gehörst zu denen, die nichts Höheres kennen, als dieses Glück, das auf der Fingerspitze Platz hat—und findet! Ich auch! Darum: Glückliche Weihnachten—aber auch etwas dazu, das man sich nicht aus der Fingerspitze saugen muss. Herzlichst, Dein Arnold Schoenberg. Weihnachten, 1921."

Other works by Arnold Schoenberg in printed scores and facsimile reproductions: *Pelleas und Melisande,* Opus 5; *Sechs Orchester-Lieder,* Opus 8, orchestral score; "Voll jener Süsse," Opus 8, No. 5, voice-piano score by Webern; *Zweites Streichquartett,* Opus 10, arranged for piano, four hands, by Felix Greissle; *Herzgewächse,* Opus 20; *Von Heute auf Morgen,* Opus 32.

Anton Bruckner. *Symphonie Nr. 7.* Deluxe edition of the full score, with embossed dedication: "Dr. Anton Webern zur Erinnerung an das Arbeiter Sinfoniekonzert 8. Jänner 1928 überreicht von der Sozialdemokratischen Kunststelle Wien, V., Sonnenhofgasse Nr. 6." On verso of title page, Webern's autograph note: "Dirigiert: 3. V. 36 (London, BBC)." Webern's annotations in colored pencil appear throughout the score.

Other conductor's scores used by Webern and containing his autograph annotations: (1) L. v. Beethoven, *Klavier-Konzert No. 5,* pocket score. Listing Vienna and Barcelona performances, 1931-32, with E. Steuermann as soloist. Copious annotations throughout. (2) F. Schubert, *Rosamunde: Zwischenakts-Musik und Ballett-Musik,* pocket score. Recording the BBC performance of 1931, and containing numerous markings. (3) J. Strauss, *An der schönen; blauen Donau,* pocket score. Listing a Vienna performance in 1930, and containing conductor's markings. (4) H. Wolf, *Italienische Serenade,* pocket score. With various dynamic markings.

Printed music bearing Webern's autograph markings, ranging from signatures of ownership to indications of interpretation: J. S. Bach, *Das wohltemperirte Clavier;* L. v. Beethoven, *Sonaten,* for pianoforte; F. Chopin, *Sonaten;* M. Clementi, *Gradus ad Parnassum II;* F. Mendelssohn, *Lieder ohne Worte;* F. Schubert, *Tänze;* R. Schumann, *Album für die Jugend;* R. Wagner, *Götterdämmerung; Tannhäuser.*

Printed copies of compositions dedicated to Webern: Hanns Eisler, *Sechs Lieder,* Opus 2; Ludwig Zenk, *Klaviersonate,* Opus 1.

Presentation copies: Hans Erich Apostel, *Fünf Lieder,* Opus 3, with the composer's autograph dedication to Webern (October 14, 1931); Theodor Streicher, *Zwanzig Lieder,* with autograph dedication to Webern by his fellow student Carl Horwitz (December 3, 1903).

Other printed scores: J. S. Bach, *B-minor Mass* and *St. Matthew Passion;* A. Berg, *Wozzeck* (fragment); A. Bruckner, *Abendzauber* (fragment); H. Eisler, *Klavierstücke,* Opus 3, *Drei Männerchöre,* Opus 10, and *Zwei Stücke für Männerchor,* Opus 19; F. Liszt, *Faust-Symphonie;* J. Haydn, *Sonaten II,* for pianoforte, and *Streichquartett,* Opus 74, No. 3; M. Reger,

Psalm 100, Opus 106; B. Romberg, *Violoncell-Concert No. 2;* F. Schubert, *Deutsche Tänze* and *Lieder und Gesänge;* Th. Streicher, *Aus des Knaben Wunderhorn;* R. Wagner, *Die Meistersinger,* Act III. Miscellaneous other scores.

Books

J. W. von Goethe. *Farbenlehre*. Pocket edition which Webern is known to have carried with him during the last period of his life. Important passages are underscored in his hand. Included are pressed alpine flowers and a photograph of Webern's wife Wilhelmine, carrying a child on her arm.

Richard Wagner an Mathilde Wesendonck. With Webern's autograph quotation entered in front of book: ". . . So komme, was da kommen mag! So lang du lebest, ist es Tag. . . ." Dated Autumn, 1904.

Matthias Claudius. *Des Wandsbecker Boten Gedichte*. Dated in Webern's hand on verso of flyleaf: "2. VII. 1922." On back flyleaf, inscription by Webern's daughter Maria Halbich: "Einem sehr lieben Menschen ein mir sehr wertvolles Buch."

Five more books with annotations in Webern's hand: K. Hildebrandt, *Hölderlin;* G. W. Leibniz, *Deutsche Schriften II; Luthers Dichtungen;* M. Maeterlinck, *L'Oiseau bleu;* O. Wilde, *Der junge König*.

Presentation copies, with inscriptions to Webern

Richard Dehmel. *Ausgewählte Gedichte.* With autograph dedication: "S/l. Toni für Compositionsversuche zum 4/XII 1901. Ernst." (Ernst Diez.) This volume contains a bookplate imprinted "Toni von Webern."

Ferdinand Avenarius. *Hausbuch deutscher Lyrik*. With autograph dedication: "Ihrem l. Toni—Minnerl, im Sept. 1904." (Wilhelmine Mörtl.) With Webern's *ex libris* as above. Pressed flowers between the leaves.

August Strindberg. *Historische Miniaturen.* Marked "Weihnachten 1908 R." A gift from Webern's sister Rosa.

Herta Staub. *Gedichte: Schaukelpferd.* With autograph dedication: "Herrn Dr. Anton v. Webern in treuer Verehrung gewidmet. Herta Staub, Wien, Nov. 1933."

Books of special significance

Bruno Wille. *Offenbarungen des Wachholderbaums.* This volume contains the quotation from Jacob Böhme which served Webern as motto for his *String Quartet* (1905), as well as the poem "Im Sommerwinde" which inspired the symphonic idyll for large orchestra (1904).

August Strindberg. *Ein Blaubuch.* This volume was extensively used by Webern; miscellaneous loose-leaf notes and numerous pressed flowers were found inserted between the pages. This is one of seven books by Strindberg in Webern's library, now preserved in the archive. Also a *feuilleton* clipping, "Im Strindberg-Turm," March, 1914, with a penciled message on the margin written and signed by Alban Berg.

Books on music

J. Hijman. *Nieuwe Oostenrijkse Muziek (Schönberg, Berg, Webern).* Treats Webern's music through Opus 22.

J. Sittard. *L. v. Beethoven: Missa solemnis.* Analysis.

R. Stöhr. *Formenlehre der Musik.*

P. Wolfrum. *Joh. Seb. Bach, Band XIII-XIV, Die Musik.*

Other books

Peter Altenberg and Alfons Canciani, special issue of *Kunst,* with nine *feuilleton* articles by Altenberg inserted by Webern in the volume; F. Avenarius, *Lebe!;* H. de Balzac, *Ursula Mirouet* and *Der Vetter Pons;* H. S. Chamberlain, *Immanuel Kant;* J. P. Eckermann, *Gespräche mit Goethe (1823-1832);* K. Hildebrandt, *Platon;* J. J. Rousseau, *Bekenntnisse I.* Miscellaneous books on philosophy, politics, and art.

Thirteen tourist guidebooks and three maps, used by Webern on his travels and mountain climbs. Some contain autograph notes. Also six mountain photographs, 23 x 17 cm.

Large map of Austria under the Hapsburg monarchy. With handwritten entries of positions and borderlines, probably dating from World War I.

A few materials from Webern's library, listed above, are damaged or incomplete through the effects of war. For example, out of the hard cover of the art book, *Die chinesische Landschaftsmalerei,* an inlay sole was cut, obviously to fill some urgent need. Exposure to the elements has affected other materials.

VII. PERSONAL RELICS

Violoncello. Used by Webern throughout his life. Damaged during the occupation of Vienna in 1945, the cello's front section was later repaired. With three fragments of the broken portion.

Woolen shawl. This brown-and-white checkered shawl has been pictured frequently in photographs showing Webern during his later years. His daughter Amalie presented it to him on Christmas, 1935, the year of her marriage to Gunther Waller.

Spectacles. The rimmed glasses which were worn by Webern to the last, and with which he is pictured in most photographs. With the black container in which Webern used to keep the glasses.

Large billfold, made of brown crocodile leather. This billfold was carried by Webern in his coat pocket to contain passport, banknotes, and other papers.

Pocket knife with etui. The knife, equipped with several blades and scissors, was used by Webern for making erasures during work at his desk, according to his daughter Amalie. The leather etui shows signs of much wear.

Cigarette case. A small etui made of brown leather over a metal frame. This and the foregoing objects were in daily use by Webern up to his death. The state of preservation of Webern's personal belongings attests to his meticulous care.

Miniature portrait of Josef Eduard von Webern (1778-1831). Painted in oil on ivory, oval-shaped, in original frame. The name is given in Gothic script on the verso of the matting, a cutout section from an old primer. Anton von Webern kept this picture of his great-grandfather above his work table, frequently pointing it out to his children as a link with their noble ancestry.

Pewter plate and silver napkin ring. Given by Webern to his son Peter, these utensils stem from the composer's mother, Amalie Geer, and belonged to the family household at the Pregelhof. The napkin ring is initialed "A. G.," the pewter plate "G. W."

Travel bag. A large leather suitcase inherited by Webern from his father and used by him on all his journeys.

VIII. ART OBJECTS

"Anton von Webern." Portrait bust, 1928. The original terra-cotta head sculptured from life by Josef Humplik. Bronze casts of this sculpture can be seen in the Historisches Museum der Stadt Wien and in the Oesterreichische Staatsgalerie. A reproduction is found in the special Webern issue of *Die Reihe* (No. II).

"Anton von Webern." Another portrait bust by Josef Humplik, differing from the foregoing. This plaster cast stood in Webern's home and was salvaged from the remnants of the household at the time of the occupation of Vienna in 1945.

"Gustav Mahler." Portrait bust, over life-size, by Josef Humplik. This plaster cast is mentioned in Webern's letter of December 29, 1929, to Josef Humplik and Hildegard Jone. It occupied a prominent place in the Webern home and was also salvaged in 1945.

"Webern in der Haustüre stehend, wenige Augenblicke vor seinem gewaltsamen Ende" ("Webern standing in the doorway of his home, a few moments before his violent end"). Original oil painting by Hildegard Jone, 1945. Reproduced in various publications, including the Webern issue of *Die Reihe,* and in Moldenhauer, *The Death of Anton Webern.* In original frame. Size of painting (without frame), 69 x 51 cm.

"Anton v. Webern vor der Todestüre." Original drawing by Hildegard Jone. Preparatory study of Webern's head for the oil painting described above.

"Anton von Webern." Original lithograph by Hildegard Jone. Engraved below the portrait is a musical quotation of the choral passage, "Freundselig ist das Wort," from the *Second Cantata,* Opus 31, written in Webern's hand and with his signature.

Original design of the first wooden cross placed on Webern's grave, drawn by Josef Humplik. Initialed and dated: "J. H., Jan. 1946."

"Anton von Webern." Original woodcut by Franz Rederer, 1964. Signed by the artist, who had drawn Webern from life in 1933.

Anton von Webern Memorial Plaque. Plaster cast of the bronze plaque, created by Anna Mahler, which was donated by the International Webern Society and unveiled at Mittersill on August 5, 1965. Dimensions: 63 x 63 cm. With the blue cloth used during the dedication ceremony.

Other art objects relating to the Webern Archive: (1) "Hildegard Jone," bronze portrait bust by Josef Humplik, one of several busts which the sculptor created of his wife, mounted on a fragment from an ancient Greek column; (2) "Self Portrait," original drawing by Hildegard Jone; (3) "Josef Humplik," original drawing by Hildegard Jone; (4) "Arnold Schoenberg," original oil portrait by Hildegard Jone; (5) "Arnold Schoenberg," four original drawings by Hildegard Jone, showing Schoenberg in various poses and bearing literary quotations; (6) "Arnold Schoenberg 1874–1951," original bronze plaque by Josef Humplik, which became the prize-winning model for the Schoenberg medal; (7) "Alban Berg," original oil portrait by Hildegard Jone; (8) "Alban Berg," two original drawings by Hildegard Jone.

IX. ASSOCIATION AND REFERENCE MATERIALS (SELECTED)

Citation and Decree of Nobility conferred upon Georg von Webern, dated May 20, 1705. Typed copy. 4 pp., 4°, narrow spaced. The original decree is in the Adelsarchiv, Vienna.

Excerpts from the records of the parish church at Salurn, referring to members of the Webern family. Typescript. 3 pp., 4°.

Obituary of Dr. h. c. Carl Webern, Anton von Webern's father. Photostat of the lengthy article in *Montanistische Rundschau.* With picture.

Memoirs (1963) of Rosa Warto, Anton von Webern's younger sister, describing details of the composer's youth. Autograph. 4 pp., 4°.

Stella Eisner. Recollections of Anton von Webern, excerpted from her memoirs. Autograph. 5 pp., 4°.

Complete record of subjects covered and grades attained by Webern during his attendance (1894-1902) at the Klagenfurt Gymnasium.

Record of academic courses and their professors at the University of Vienna during Webern's matriculation (1902-6).

Excerpts from Webern's letters (1900-34) to his cousin Ernst Diez, compiled by Amalie Waller. Typescript. 6 pp.

Microfilm of Webern's sixteen letters (1910-13) to the Viennese composer Paul Königer.

Facsimile reproduction of fifteen letters from Webern to Alexander von Zemlinsky (1912-32). 29 pp.

Facsimile reproduction of a letter from Webern to Arnold Schoenberg (Stettin, January 13, 1913). 4 pp.

Twenty-one original programs of concerts conducted by Webern (1922-33).

File of newspaper articles pertaining to the Workmen's Symphony and Singverein concerts conducted by Webern (1926-32). Also Johann Humpelstetter's membership card in the Singverein and podium card for the performance of Mahler's *Eighth Symphony* under Webern.

Johann Humpelstetter. "Anton Webern als nachschaffender Künstler, als Chorleiter und Dirigent." Personal recollections by a chorus member of the Singverein der Kunststelle, covering the years 1926-34. Original typescript. 23 pp., 4°. Also miscellaneous related notes. Autograph. 5 pp.

Adolph Weiss. "Recollections of Anton von Webern." Typed transcript of a recorded interview, conducted by William George. 4 pp., 4°.

Werner Riemerschmid. "Bericht über die Bergung von Briefen, Manuskripten und anderen Dingen, die zum Eigentum Anton von Weberns gehörten." Dr. Riemerschmid's report on his initiative, late in 1945, involving the salvaging of Webern's letters, manuscripts, and other materials. With typed copies of four letters written by Webern to Riemerschmid during 1944 regarding a recitation of Hildegard Jone's poems set to music by Webern. Typescript. 9 pp., 4°.

Facsimile reproduction of a letter from Webern to the editor of *Muziek* in Amsterdam (1930). 1 p.

Copies of nine letters from Webern to Roberto Gerhard (1931-34). Typescript. 10 pp., 4°.

Special Webern issue of the Viennese periodical "*23*" on the occasion of Webern's fiftieth birthday. Issue No. 14, published February, 1934. Also proofsheets with copious autograph annotations by the editor, Alban Berg.

"Ueber musikalische Formen, Formenlehre an Hand von Analysen." Notebook kept by Rudolf Schopf during Webern's Beethoven lectures given between December 14, 1934, and April 4, 1935, at the home of Dr. Rudolf Kurzmann, Vienna.

With numerous direct quotations of Webern's statements and copious musical examples from Beethoven's piano sonatas. Autograph. 99 pp., 4°.

Georg Trakl. "Die Sonne." Text of the first poem in Webern's cycle of *Trakl Lieder*, Opus 14, in Trakl's autograph. 1 p., 4°. The manuscript formerly belonged to Hildegard Jone.

Hildegard Jone. Three unpublished cycles of poems: (1) "Enthüllte Form." Autograph. 10 pp., 4°. (2) "Lumen," which provided the textual source for Webern's last unfinished composition. Autograph. 15 pp., 4° and 8°. (3) "Requiem in memoriam Anton von Webern." Autograph. 6 pp., various sizes.

"Stellen, die Anton Webern aus der Farbenlehre Goethes abgeschrieben hat." Hildegard Jone's autograph copy of passages from Goethe's *Farbenlehre* which had been excerpted by Webern. 9 pp., 8°.

Facsimile reproduction of five letters from Webern to Erwin Stein (1938-39). 10 pp. Also typed copy of Webern's own analysis of his *Quartet*, Opus 28. 5 pp., 4°, narrow spaced.

Facsimile reproduction: "Abtretung des Urheberrechtes." Contract between Universal Edition and Wilhelmine von Webern for the posthumous Opera 17, 24, 25, 29, 30, and 31. 1945.

Facsimile reproduction: Agreement between Bomart Music Publications and Wilhelmine von Webern concerning the *Quintet* (1906). 1949.

Luigi Dallapiccola. "Incontro con Anton Webern (Pagine di diario)." [Published in an abridged version in *Il Mondo* (Florence), November 11, 1945.] Complete original typescript. 5 pp., 4°. With English translation by Mario Castelnuovo-Tedesco in the translator's autograph. 10 pp., 4°.

Festival address by Dr. Josef Polnauer on the occasion of the unveiling of memorial plaques for Schoenberg and Webern in Mödling (1959). Typescript. 8 pp., 4°.

Humphrey Searle. "Anton Webern." [Essay published in an

abridged version in the *Sunday Telegraph* (London), April 16, 1961, under the title "Webern—the Evolutionist."] Complete autograph manuscript. 6 pp., 4°.

Ernst Krenek. Three Webern lectures: (1) "Anton Webern, Profile." [Published in the present volume.] Autograph manuscript. 19 pp., 4°. (2) "Analysis of Symphony, Opus 21." Unpublished autograph manuscript. 14 pp., 4°. (3) "Anton Weberns magisches Quadrat." Address delivered at the unveiling of the Webern Memorial Plaque at Mittersill on August 5, 1965. [Published in *Forum*, August–September, 1965.] Autograph manuscript. 4 pp., 4°. Also a tape recording of this address made by Radio Salzburg during the unveiling ceremony.

Complete file of correspondence and documentation covering research into the circumstances of Webern's death.

File of documentation for a projected biography, "Anton von Webern: Path and Prophecy," by Hans Moldenhauer.

Archive of the First International Webern Festival (University of Washington, Seattle, 1962). A file of materials preparatory to, and emanating from, the festival: programs, magazine and newspaper articles, correspondence, photographs, and tapes of all festival concerts.

Archive of the International Webern Society. A file of organizational material, including correspondence with all of the charter members and the minutes of the organizational meeting.

File of documentation for the Second International Webern Festival at Salzburg/Mittersill, August 2-5, 1965 (Salzburg Festival and International Webern Society). Programs, newspaper articles, correspondence.

Heinrich Strobel. "So sehe ich Webern." Festival address delivered at the first of three Webern Memorial Concerts during the Salzburg Festival (Mozarteum, August 2-3, 1965). Original typescript, inscribed to the Webern Archive by the author. Salzburg, August 2, 1965. 10 pp., 4°. Published in *Melos*, September, 1965.

Peter Ehrenstrasser. "In Memoriam." Address given at the Webern Memorial Concert in St. Anna Chapel, Mittersill, on August 4, 1965, by the priest who had buried Webern in 1945. Autograph manuscript. 1 p., 4°.

Anton von Webern Memorial Program, directed by Cesar Bresgen. Tape recording of a broadcast over Radio Salzburg on September 15, 1965. With many musical examples and literary quotations.

Various association items relating to Hildegard Jone, Josef Humplik, Georg Trakl, Edwin Komauer (Webern's teacher at Klagenfurt), Rudolph Ganz, Franz Rederer, and others.

Webern Reference Library of publications since 1912. Books, essays, programs, newspaper articles, scores, recordings, and related materials.

Addendum: Received too late for detailed description in this catalogue were documents and relics from the estate of Guido von Webern (1888-1962), the composer's cousin. These items include, among others: original Decree of Nobility, bestowed by Emperor Charles VI in 1731, containing family history and colored coat of arms; oil miniature of a male ancestor; engraving done by Josef Eduard von Webern (1830); large album with ornate metal coat of arms, once belonging to the composer's grandfather Anton, with 121 family portraits; signet (metal stamp with coat of arms); various family documents and letters dating back to 1643.

Selected Bibliography

The following selective list is designed to serve as a guide to further study, depending upon the reader's background and interests. The items vary in content from comparatively non-technical introductions (Collaer; Demuth; Hamilton; Hodeir; Machlis; Searle) through a spectrum of increasingly technical discussions of a theoretical or analytical nature.

For extensive bibliographies of the literature to about 1961, see Basart (serial music) and Kolneder (Webern).

For any fuller understanding of Webern's music, one should be acquainted with at least the basic treatises on twelve-tone technique by Perle, Rochberg, and Rufer.

The publications listed under "Periodicals" are in general rewarding for discussions of contemporary music in its various aspects.

Also here included are some other writings by the contributors to this present volume (listed under their names); some articles pertinent to the First International Webern Festival; and a few other recent books and dissertations of general interest.

Austin, William. "The Idea of Evolution in the Music of the 20th Century," *Musical Quarterly,* XXXIX (January, 1953), 26-36.

———. *Music in the 20th Century: From Debussy through Stravinsky.* New York: W. W. Norton, 1966.

Babbitt, Milton. "Some Aspects of Twelve-Tone Composition," *Score*, No. 12 (June, 1955), pp. 53-61.
An account of developments in the United States.

———. "Twelve-Tone Invariants as Compositional Determinants," in *Problems of Modern Music, Musical Quarterly*, XLVI (April, 1960), 246-59.

———. "Set Structure as a Compositional Determinant," *Journal of Music Theory*, V (1961), 72-94.

———. "Twelve-Tone Rhythmic Structure and the Electronic Medium," *Perspectives of New Music*, I (1962), 49-79.

Basart, Ann Phillips. *Serial Music: A Classified Bibliography of Writings on Twelve-Tone and Electronic Music*. Berkeley and Los Angeles: University of California Press, 1961. xiii, 151 pp.
An important guide to the literature, with 823 items listed and annotated. Sections devoted to the Viennese School (Schoenberg, Berg, Webern), and to Milton Babbitt, Luciano Berio, Pierre Boulez, John Cage, Luigi Dallapiccola, Wolfgang Fortner, Roberto Gerhard, Josef Matthias Hauer, Hans Werner Henze, Hanns Jelinek, Giselher Klebe, Ernst Krenek, René Leibowitz, Bruno Maderna, Luigi Nono, Henri Pousseur, Humphrey Searle, Mátyás Seiber, Karlheinz Stockhausen, Igor Stravinsky. New edition in preparation.

Beale, James. "Weberns musikalischer Nachlass," *Melos*, XXXI (October, 1964), 297-303.

Beale, Jane Guthrie. "An Archive for Webern," *The Music Magazine* (Evanston, Ill.), CLXIV (February, 1962), 13-14.

Bradshaw, Merrill K. Tonal Structure in the Early Works of Anton Webern. . . . Ph.D. thesis, University of Illinois, 1962. 295 pp. in 2 vols. Ann Arbor, Mich.: University Microfilms, No. 62-6106.
Discussion of Webern Opera 1-5; with an original composition by the author, *Orchestra M[illegible]c in Five Movements (1959-1962)*.

Bresgen, Cesar. "Anton Webern in Mittersill," *Oesterreichische Musikzeitschrift*, XVI (May, 1961), 226-28.

Briner, Andres. "An den Wurzeln eines neuen musikalischen Stils; zu einer Vortragsreihe von Anton v. Webern," *Schweizerische Musikzeitung* (Zurich), CI (1961), 15-20.

Broekema, Andrew J. A Stylistic Analysis and Comparison of the Solo Vocal Works of Arnold Schoenberg, Alban Berg, and Anton Webern. Ph.D. thesis, University of Texas, 1962. 351 pp. Ann Arbor, Mich.: University Microfilms, No. 62-4822.

Castiglioni, Niccolò. "Sul rapporto tra parola e musica nella seconda Cantata di Webern," *Incontri musicali*, No. 3 (August, 1959), pp. 112-27.

Chicago Symphony Orchestra Program Notes, January 31, 1963, pp. 15-21.

Webern's *Passacaglia* discussed by Arnold Parsons.

Collaer, Paul. "Arnold Schoenberg, Anton Webern, and Alban Berg," in *A History of Modern Music*, translated by Sally Abeles from the second edition of the French text, *La musique moderne* (Brussels: Elsevier, 1955), chap. ii, pp. 58-114. Cleveland: World Publishing Co., 1961. 414 pp.; 134 musical examples.

Cowell, Henry. "Current Chronicle: New York," *Musical Quarterly*, XXXV (January, 1949), 106-11.

A review of Schoenberg's *Five Orchestral Pieces* and Webern's *Passacaglia*.

Craft, Robert. "Discoveries and Convictions," *Counterpoint*, XVIII (February, 1953), 16-18.

Review of an all-Webern concert by ISCM.

———. "Anton Webern," *Score*, No. 13 (September, 1953), pp. 9-22.

Includes a list of the compositions, with timings.

———. See also under *Webern: The Complete Music*.

Demuth, Norman. "Anton von Webern," in *Musical Trends in*

the 20th Century, chap. ix, pp. 233-38. London: Rockliff, 1952. xvii, 359 pp.

Döhl, Friedhelm. "Weberns Opus 27," *Melos,* XXX (December, 1963), 400-3.

———. "Die Welt der Dichtung in Weberns Musik," *Melos,* XXXI (March, 1964), 88-90.

Dorian, Frederick Deutsch. "Webern als Lehrer," *Melos,* XXVII (April, 1960), 101-6.

Eimert, Herbert. "Die Reihe, das unbekannte Wesen," *Melos,* XXIX (July–August, 1962), 219-22.

Elston, Arnold. "Some Rhythmic Practices in Contemporary Music," *Musical Quarterly,* XLII (July, 1956), 318-29.
Discussion of Webern's Opus 22, pp. 325-29.

Erhardt, Ludwik. "W strone Weberna," *Ruch Muzyczny* (Warsaw), V (1961), 18-19.

Fortner, Wolfgang. "Anton Webern und unsere Zeit," *Melos,* XXVII (November, 1960), 325-27.

Friedheim, Philip. Tonality and Structure in the Early Works of Schoenberg. Ph.D. thesis, New York University, 1963. 557 pp.

Gerhard, Roberto, ed. "Letters of Webern and Schoenberg," *Score,* No. 24 (November, 1958), pp. 36-41.
Includes texts of six letters from Webern to Gerhard: December 22, 1931; January 13, 1932; May 6, 1932; February 4, 1933; June 26, 1933; May 21, 1934.

Goléa, Antoine. *Vingt ans de musique contemporaine.* Paris: Segher. Reviewed by Helmut Lohmüller in *Melos,* XXX (April, 1963), 123-24.

Hamilton, Iain. "Alban Berg and Anton Webern," in *European Music in the Twentieth Century,* ed. Howard Hartog, pp. 94-117. London: Routledge and Kegan Paul; New York: Frederick A. Praeger, 1957. 341 pp.

Hansen, Peter S. "Berg and Webern," in *An Introduction to*

Twentieth Century Music, chap. xi, pp. 197-219. Boston: Allyn and Bacon, 1961. 376 pp.

Hodeir, André. "Anton Webern," in *Since Debussy: A View of Contemporary Music*, trans. Noel Burch, chap. iv, pp. 69-80. New York: Grove Press, 1961. 256 pp.

Irino, Yoshio. ["Webern's Concerto for Nine Instruments"], *Ongaku-Geijutsu* [*Music-Art*] (Tokyo), XII, No. 1 (1954), 26.
A thematic and structural analysis of Opus 24.

Jelinek, Hanns. *Anleitung zur Zwölftonkomposition*. Vienna: Universal Edition, 1952. 106 pp.
Reviewed by Ernst Krenek in *Musical Quarterly*, XL (April, 1954), 250-56; by Dika Newlin in *Notes*, XVII (1960), 245.

Karkoschka, Erhard. Zur Entwicklung der Kompositionstechnik im Frühwerk Anton Weberns. Ph.D. thesis, Tübingen, 1959.
Listed in Kolneder.

Koegler, Horst. "Choreographen adaptieren moderne Musik," *Melos*, XXVIII (April, 1961), 105-6.
An account of choreographic use of Webern's Op. 6 and Op. 10.

Kolneder, Walter. *Anton Webern: Einführung in Werk und Stil.* (Kontrapunkte: Schriften zur deutschen Musik der Gegenwart, ed. Heinrich Lindlar, Vol. V.) Rodenkirchen am Rhein: P. J. Tonger, 1961. 195 pp.
Contains a bibliography of 233 items, pp. 184-92. Reviewed by Dika Newlin in *Journal of the American Musicological Society*, XVI (1963), 266-69.

Krenek, Ernst. "Freiheit und Verantwortung," in *23, eine Wiener Musikzeitschrift*, No. 14 (February, 1934), pp. 10-11.

———. "Apologie," *Wiener Zeitung*, January 1-5, 1935.

———. *Ueber neue Musik: Sechs Vorlesungen zur Einführung in die theoretischen Grundlagen*. Vienna: Ringbuchhandlung, 1937. 108 pp.

———. *Selbstdarstellung*. Zurich: Atlantis, 1948. 66 pp. Revised and enlarged as "Self-Analysis," in *New Mexico Quarterly*, XXIII (Spring, 1953), 5-57, with catalogue of works and discography.

———. *Zwölfton-Kontrapunkt-Studien*. Mainz: B. Schott's Söhne, 1952.

———. "Is the Twelve-Tone Technique on the Decline?" *Musical Quarterly*, XXXIX (October, 1953), 513-27.

———. *De rebus prius factis*. Frankfurt am Main: Wilhelm Hansen Musikverlag, 1956.

———. "Vom Altern und Veralten der Musik," *Forum*, III (December, 1956), 446-48.

———. "Der ganze Webern in drei Stunden," *Melos*, XXIV (1957), 304 ff.

———. "Bericht über Versuche in total determinierter Musik," *Darmstädter Beiträge*, I (1958), 17-21.

———. "Vom Verfall des Einfalls," in *Prisma der gegenwärtigen Musik*, pp. 137-44. Hamburg, 1959.

———. "Extents and Limits of Serial Techniques," in *Problems of Modern Music, Musical Quarterly*, XLVI (April, 1960), 210-32.

———. "Bemerkungen zur Wiener Schule," *Oesterreichische Musikzeitschrift*, XVII (April, 1962), 184 ff.

———. "Hol' der Henker eure beiden Häuser!" *Forum*, XI (January-February, 1964), 43-46, 106-9.

Lang, Paul Henry. "Editorial," *Musical Quarterly*, XLIV (October, 1958), 503-10.

Discusses the place and role of dodecaphony in present and future music.

Leibowitz, René. *Schoenberg et son école*. Paris: J. B. Janin, 1947. 302 pp.

———. *Qu'est ce que la musique de douze sons? Le Concerto pour neuf instruments, op. 24, d'Anton Webern*. Liège: Editions Dynamo, 1948. 63 pp.

This and the preceding work are reviewed by Milton Babbitt in *Journal of the American Musicological Society,* III (1950), 57-60.

Lewin, David. "A Metrical Problem in Webern's Op. 27," *Journal of Music Theory,* VI (1962), 124-32.

Ligeti, György. "Die Komposition mit Reihen und ihre Konsequenzen bei Anton Webern," *Oesterreichische Musikzeitschrift,* XVI (June-July, 1961), 297-302.

———. *Einführung in die Musik von Anton Webern.* Vienna: Universal Edition, in preparation.

Machlis, Joseph. "Anton Webern" (chap. lviii), and "Three Works by Webern" (chap. lvix), in *Introduction to Contemporary Music,* pp. 383-403. New York: W. W. Norton, 1961. xxiii, 714 pp.

McKenzie, Wallace C., Jr. The Music of Anton Webern. Ph.D. thesis, North Texas State College, 1960. 507 pp. Ann Arbor: University Microfilms, No. 60-2792.

Malipiero, Riccardo. *Guida alla dodecafonia.* (Piccola Biblioteca Ricordi, 15.) Milan: Ricordi, 1961. 114 pp.

Martino, Donald. "The Source Set and Its Aggregate Formations," *Journal of Music Theory,* V (1961), 224-73.

Mason, Colin. "Webern's Later Chamber Music," *Music and Letters,* XXXVIII (July, 1957), 232-37.
Discussion of Opera 22, 24, 28.

Matsudaira, Yoriaki. ["After Webern"], *Ongaku-Geijutsu* [*Music-Art*] (Tokyo), XX, No. 1 (1962), 37.

Moldenhauer, Hans. *The Death of Anton Webern: A Drama in Documents.* New York: Philosophical Library, 1961. 118 pp.
A clarification of the circumstances surrounding the composer's violent death on September 15, 1945.

———. *Anton von Webern: Path and Prophecy.* [A biography.] In preparation.

———. "The Last Evening of Anton Webern's Life," *New York Times,* December 25, 1960, Section X, p. 11.

———. "Rich Webern Legacy Contains Unknown Compositions," *New York Times,* September 17, 1961, Section X, p. 11.

———. "Wealth of Webern Manuscripts Now at University of Washington," *Music of the West Magazine* (Los Angeles), XVII (November, 1961), 11-13.

———. "First International Webern Festival to Be Held in Seattle," *Music of the West Magazine,* XVII (April, 1962), 4-5.

"Moldenhauer Archive Gets Anton Webern's Writings," *Music of the West Magazine,* XVII (October, 1961), 10.

Moroi, Makoto. ["A Study on Webern"] *Ongaku-Geijutsu* [*Music-Art*], (Tokyo), Vol. XIX (1961), No. 1, p. 40; No. 3, p. 22; No. 5, p. 26; No. 6, p. 20; No. 7, p. 19; No. 9, p. 18; No. 10, p. 38; No. 11, p. 42; No. 12, p. 24; Vol. XX (1962), No. 2, p. 10; No. 3, p. 20; No. 5, p. 28; No. 6, p. 47.

A row and structural analysis of Webern's Opera 10, 17, 18, 19, 20, 21, 22.

Myers, Rollo Hugh, ed. *Twentieth Century Music.* London: Calder, 1960. 243 pp.

Nelson, Robert U. "Schoenberg's Variation Seminar," *Musical Quarterly,* L (April, 1964), 141-64.

Odegard, Peter S. The Variation Sets of Arnold Schoenberg. Ph.D. thesis, University of California (Berkeley), 1964. 510 pp.

Oehlmann, Werner. *Die Musik des 20. Jahrhunderts.* Berlin: De Gruyter, 1961. 312 pp.

Ogdon, Wilbur Lee. Series and Structure: An Investigation into the Purpose of the Twelve-Note Row in Selected Works of Schoenberg, Webern, Krenek, and Leibowitz. Ph.D. thesis, Indiana University, 1955. Ann Arbor: University Microfilms, No. 14663.

Includes a row analysis of Webern's Opus 27.

———. "A Webern Analysis," *Journal of Music Theory,* VI (1962), 133-38.

Discussion of the *Variations for Piano*, Opus 27.

Parmenter, Ross. "Webern's Torch Will Burn in Seattle as Devotees Plan to Honor Him," *New York Times*, April 29, 1962, Section X, p. 9.

A report on preparations for the First International Webern Festival.

Perle, George. "Atonality and the Twelve-Tone System in the United States," *Score*, No. 27 (July, 1960), pp. 51-66.

———. *Serial Composition and Atonality: An Introduction to the Music of Schoenberg, Berg and Webern*. Berkeley and Los Angeles: University of California Press, 1962. 154 pp.

Numerous musical excerpts are analyzed and explained in relation to the "sets" (tone rows) involved.

———. "*Lulu:* The Formal Design," *Journal of the American Musicological Society*, XVII (1964), 179-92.

Philadelphia Orchestra Program Notes, February 15, 1963, pp. 16-22.

Webern's *Im Sommerwind* discussed by Edwin H. Schloss and Max de Schaunsee.

Pisk, Paul A. "Schoenberg's Twelve-Tone Opera," *Modern Music*, VII (April–May, 1930), 18-21. Reprinted in *Schoenberg*, ed. Merle Armitage, pp. 187-94. New York: G. Schirmer, 1937.

———. "Anton Webern: Profile of a Composer," *Texas Quarterly* (Winter, 1962), pp. 114-20.

———. "Seattle: Auch von Webern gibt es noch Uraufführungen," *Melos*, XXIX (July–August, 1962), 252-53.

A brief account of the First International Webern Festival.

Plebe, Armando. *La dodecafonia; documenti e pagine critiche.* (Biblioteca di cultura moderna, 574.) Bari: Editori Laterza, 1962. 230 pp.

Polnauer, Josef, ed. [Letters of Webern and Berg.] Vienna: Universal Edition, in preparation.

———. See also under Webern.

Pousseur, Henri. "Webern und die Theorie," *Darmstädter Beiträge,* I (1958), 38-43.

Prieberg, Fred K. *Lexikon der neuen Musik.* Freiberg: Karl Alber, 1958. 495 pp.

Problems of Modern Music: The Princeton Seminar in Advanced Musical Studies, Musical Quarterly (special issue), XLVI (April, 1960), 145-259. Reprinted as a separate volume, ed. Paul Henry Lang. New York: W. W. Norton, 1962. 121 pp.

Redlich, Hans Ferdinand. *Alban Berg: The Man and His Music.* New York: Abelard-Schuman, 1957. 316 pp.

———. "Anton von Webern," in *Die Musik in Geschichte und Gegenwart,* Vol. XIV. Kassel: Bärenreiter, in preparation.

Reich, Willi. *Alban Berg: Leben und Werk.* Zurich: Atlantis Verlag, 1963. 215 pp.

———. "Anton Webern über Alban Berg," *Neue Zeitschrift für Musik,* CXXIV (1963), 143.

———, ed. *Alban Berg, Bildnis im Wort: Selbstzeugnisse und Aussagen der Freunde.* Zurich: Die Arche, 1959. 89 pp.

———, ed. *Anton Webern: Weg und Gestalt; Selbstzeugnisse und Worte der Freunde.* Zurich: Verlag der Arche, 1961. 80 pp.

Ringger, Rolf Urs. "Zur Wort-Ton-Beziehung beim frühen Anton Webern; Analyse von Op. 3, Nr. 1," *Schweizerische Musikzeitung,* CIII (1963), 330-35.

Rochberg, George. *The Hexachord and Its Relation to the 12-Tone Row.* Bryn Mawr, Pa.: Theodore Presser Co., 1955. 40 pp. A monograph explaining certain aspects of the twelve-tone technique: namely, the principles of constructing a row whose two halves (hexachords) will be symmetrical through mirror inversion.

———. "Webern's Search for Harmonic Identity," *Journal of Music Theory,* VI (Spring, 1962), 109-24.

Rufer, Josef. *Composition with Twelve Notes Related Only to One Another,* translated by Humphrey Searle from the German edition, *Die Komposition mit zwölf Tönen* (Berlin: Max Hesses Verlag, 1952). New York: Macmillan Co., 1954. xiv, 218 pp., and pp. I-XXIV of musical examples.

An authoritative exposition of the methods of twelve-tone composition, based upon the compositions and theoretical writings of Schoenberg.

———. *The Works of Arnold Schoenberg: A Catalogue of His Compositions, Writings, and Paintings,* translated by Dika Newlin from the German edition, *Das Werk Arnold Schoenbergs* (Kassel: Bärenreiter, 1959; 207 pp.). London: Faber and Faber, 1962; New York: Free Press of Glencoe, 1963. 214 pp.

St. Louis Symphony Program Notes, October 20, 1962.

Webern's *Six Pieces for Orchestra,* Op. 6, discussed by Leigh Gerdine.

Salzman, Eric. "Unheard Scores of Webern Found," *New York Times,* September 4, 1961, p. 17.

San Francisco Symphony Program Notes, May 1, 1963.

Webern's *Passacaglia,* Op. 1, discussed.

Schoenberg, Arnold. *Theory of Harmony.* Translated from *Harmonielehre* [abridged] by Robert D. W. Adams. New York: Philosophical Library, 1948. 336 pp.

———. *Style and Idea.* New York: Philosophical Library, 1950. 224 pp.

———. *Structural Functions of Harmony.* London: Williams and Norgate, 1954. 200 pp.

———. *Preliminary Exercises in Counterpoint,* ed. Leonard Stein. London: Faber and Faber, 1963; New York: St. Martin's Press, 1964. 231 pp.

———. [Collected essays, edited by Leonard Stein.] In preparation.

Schollum, Robert. *Egon Wellesz.* Vienna: Oesterreichischer Bundesverlag, 1964. 80 pp.

Schonberg, Harold C. "Kindness Kills," *New York Times,* June 10, 1962, Section X, p. 11.

An account of the First International Webern Festival.

Searle, Humphrey. "Webern, Anton (von)," in *Grove's Dictionary of Music and Musicians*, X, 225-28. 5th ed. London: Macmillan and Co., 1954.

Shibata, Minao. ["Anton Webern"], *Ongaku-Geijutsu* [*Music-Art*] (Tokyo), XV, No. 8 (1957), 52.
A description of Webern's life and works.

———. [*Contemporary Composers.*] Tokyo: Ongaku-no-toma Sha, 1958. 249 pp.
Bibliographical and stylistic discussions; also a survey of twentieth-century music. Luigi Dallapiccola, pp. 103-15; Arnold Schoenberg, pp. 141-59; Alban Berg, pp. 161-75; Anton Webern, pp. 177-86.

Spinner, Leopold. "Anton Weberns Kantate Nr. 2, Opus 31; die Formprinzipien der kanonischen Darstellung," *Schweizerische Musikzeitung*, CI (1961), 303-8.

Stein, Leonard. "The *Privataufführungen* Revisited," in *Paul A. Pisk: Essays in His Honor*, ed. John Glowacki. [University of Texas, Department of Music, in preparation.]

Stockhausen, Karlheinz. "Weberns Konzert für 9 Instrumente, op. 24; Analyse des ersten Satzes," *Melos*, XX (December, 1953), 343-48.

Stravinsky, Igor. *Poetics of Music in the Form of Six Lessons*, translated from the French by Arthur Knodel and Ingolf Dahl. (Charles Eliot Norton Lectures delivered in 1939-40.) Cambridge, Mass.: Harvard University Press, 1947; New York: Vintage Books, 1956, 142 pp.

———, and Robert Craft. *Conversations with Igor Stravinsky*. Garden City, N.Y.: Doubleday and Co., 1959. 162 pp.

———, and Robert Craft. *Memories and Commentaries*. Garden City, N.Y.: Doubleday and Co., 1960. 167 pp.

———, and Robert Craft. *Expositions and Developments*. Garden City, N.Y.: Doubleday and Co., 1962, 192 pp.

———, and Robert Craft. *Dialogues and a Diary*. Garden City, N.Y.: Doubleday and Co., 1963, 288 pp.

Strobel, Heinrich. "Die Wiener Schule," *Melos*, XXX (November, 1963), 369-77.

Stuckenschmidt, Hans Heinz. *Schöpfer der neuen Musik: Portraits und Studien*. Frankfurt am Main: Suhrkamp Verlag, 1958. 301 pp. Also Munich: Deutscher Taschenbuch-Verlag, 1962. 211 pp.

Contains biographical and stylistic discussions of Stravinsky, Schoenberg, Berg, Webern (pp. 192-203), Dallapiccola, Henze.

———. "Contemporary Techniques in Music," *Musical Quarterly*, XLIX (1963), 1-16.

Swabay, John Lee. Romantic Style Characteristics Which Led to the Rise of Dodecaphonic Techniques. Ph.D. thesis, University of Texas, 1963. 413 pp. Ann Arbor: University Microfilms, No. 64-112.

Vlad, Roman. *Storia della dodecafonia*. Milan: Suvini-Zerboni, 1958. 395 pp.

A history of twelve-tone music up to Stravinsky's *Agon;* Webern, pp. 125-30.

Webern, Anton von. *Briefe an Hildegard Jone und Josef Humplik*, ed. Josef Polnauer. Vienna: Universal Edition, 1959. 106 pp.

———. *The Path to the New Music*. Translated by Leo Black from the German edition, *Der Weg zur neuen Musik*, ed. Willi Reich (Vienna: Universal Edition, 1960; 73 pp.). Bryn Mawr, Pa.: Theodore Presser Co., 1963. 67 pp.

———. *Webern: The Complete Music*, recorded under the direction of Robert Craft. Four 12-inch Columbia Records, K4L-232. With a highly informative accompanying brochure.

Reviewed by Edward A. Lippman in *Musical Quarterly*, XLIV (1958), 416-19.

———. See also under Gerhard (letters); Polnauer (letters); Reich (*Weg und Gestalt*).

Wellesz, Egon. *The Origins of Schoenberg's Twelve-Tone System.* Washington, D.C.: Library of Congress, 1958. 14 pp.

Westergaard, Peter. "Some Problems in Rhythmic Theory and Analysis," *Perspectives of New Music,* I (Fall, 1962), 180-91. Discussion of Webern's Opus 27.

———. "Webern and 'Total Organization': An Analysis of the Second Movement of Piano Variations, Op. 27," *Perspectives of New Music,* I (Spring, 1963), 107-20.

Wildberger, Jacques. "Webern gestern und heute," *Melos,* XXVII (April, 1960), 126.

Wildgans, Friedrich. "Anton von Webern; zu seinen 75. Geburtstag am 3. Dezember 1958," *Oesterreichische Musikzeitschrift,* XIII (November, 1958), 456-60.

———. "Gustav Mahler und Anton von Webern," *Oesterreichische Musikzeitschrift,* XV (June, 1960), 302-6.

PERIODICALS

Darmstädter Beiträge zur neuen Musik, ed. Wolfgang Steinecke. Mainz: Schott, 1958——.

Analysis of Vols. I (1958) and II (1959) in Basart, entries 170 and 174. Vol. III (1960), 118 pp. Vol. V (1963), 128 pp., Pierre Boulez, *Musikdenken heute.* Vol. VIII (1964), Lejaren A. Hiller, Jr., *Informationstheorie und Computermusik.*

Journal of Music Theory, ed. Allen Forte. New Haven, Conn.: School of Music, Yale University, 1957——. Semiannually.

Melos: Zeitschrift für neue Musik, ed. Heinrich Strobel. Melos-Verlag, Postfach 1403, 6500 Mainz, Germany. Monthly.

Oesterreichische Musikzeitschrift, ed. Elisabeth Lafite. Wiedner Hauptstrasse 15, Wien IV, Austria. Monthly.

Perspectives of New Music, ed. Arthur Berger. Princeton, N.J.: Princeton University Press (for the Fromm Music Foundation), 1962——. Twice yearly.

Die Reihe: Information über serielle Musik, ed. Herbert Eimert and Karlheinz Stockhausen. Vienna: Universal Edition, 1955——. American edition: *Die Reihe: A Periodical Devoted to Developments in Contemporary Music*, ed. Herbert Eimert and Karlheinz Stockhausen. Bryn Mawr, Pa.: Theodore Presser Co., 1958——.

I. *Elektronische Musik*, 1955, 63 pp. (*Electronic Music*, 1958, 62 pp.)

II. *Anton Webern: Dokumente, Bekenntnis, Erkenntnisse, Analysen*, 1955, 102 pp. (*Anton Webern*, 1958, 100 pp.) German edition reviewed by Dika Newlin in *Notes*, XIII (June, 1956), 432-33. American edition reviewed by Everett Helm in *Journal of Music Theory*, III (April, 1959), 155-60; by Dika Newlin in *Notes*, XVI (March, 1959), 257-58.

III. *Musikalisches Handwerk*, 1957, 88 pp. (*Musical Craftsmanship*, 1959, 88 pp.)

IV. *Junge Komponisten*, 1958, 133 pp. (*Young Composers*, 1960, 136 pp.)

V. *Berichte / Analysen*, 1959. (*Reports; Analyses*, 1961, 121 pp.)

VI. *Sprache und Musik*, 1960. 88 pp. (*Speech and Music*, 1964.)

VII. *Form-Raum*, 1960, 88 pp.

Schweizerische Musikzeitung, ed. Dr. Willi Schuh, Verlag Hug & Co., Limmatquai 28, Zurich 1, Switzerland. Bimonthly.

The Score: A Music Magazine, ed. William Glock. 2 Beaufort House, Beaufort Street, London, S.W. 3, England. Three issues yearly, 1949-61 (discontinued).

Reference List of Webern's Musical Works

Page references indicate mention or discussion in the present volume.

WORKS WITH OPUS NUMBERS

All of the works with opus numbers (except 13a and 14a) are published by Universal Edition A.G., Karlsplatz 6, Vienna I, Austria.

OPUS

1 *Passacaglia for Orchestra* (1908), xxv, 43, 54, 81, 90, 125, 151
3 flutes, 3 oboes, 3 clarinets, 3 bassoons, 4 horns, 3 trumpets, 3 trombones, tuba, timpani, percussion, harp, strings

2 *Entflieht auf leichten Kähnen* (Stefan George), for mixed chorus a cappella (1908), viii, ix, 16, 54, 62, 64, 76, 90, 91, 125

3 *Five Songs* (from *Der siebente Ring* by Stefan George), for medium voice and piano (1907-8), viii, 28, 55, 57, 60, 63, 125-26
(1) "Dies ist ein Lied für dich allein"
(2) "Im Windesweben war meine Frage nur Träumerei"
(3) "An Bachesranft die einzigen Frühen die Hasel blühen," 63
(4) "Im Morgentaun trittst du hervor"
(5) "Kahl reckt der Baum im Winterdunst"

4 *Five Songs* (Stefan George), for high voice and piano (1908-9), viii, ix, 28, 55, 57, 125
(1) "Welt der Gestalten, lang Lebewohl!"
(2) "Noch zwingt mich Treue über dir zu wachen"
(3) "Je Heil und Dank dir die den Segen brachte!"

(4) "So ich traurig bin, weiss ich nur ein Ding"
(5) "Ihr tratet zu dem Herde wo alle Glut verstarb"

5 *Five Movements for String Quartet* (1909), viii, ix, xxiv, xxvi, 126
Also arranged for string orchestra (1929), 126

6 *Six Pieces for Large Orchestra*, xxiv, xxv, xxvi, 81, 126-27, 151
First version (1910): 4 flutes, 4 oboes (2 English horns), 5 clarinets (2 bass clarinets), 3 bassoons (1 contrabassoon), 6 horns, 6 trumpets, 6 trombones, tuba, 3 timpani, percussion, glockenspiel, celesta, 2 harps, strings
Second version (1928): 2 flutes, 2 oboes, 3 clarinets, 2 bassoons, 4 horns, 4 trumpets, 4 trombones, tuba, timpani, percussion, glockenspiel, celesta, harp, strings

7 *Four Pieces for Violin and Piano* (1910), viii, ix, 127

8 *Two Songs* (Rainer Maria Rilke), for medium voice, clarinet (bass clarinet), horn, trumpet, celesta, harp, violin, viola, and cello (1910), viii, 63, 127
(1) "Du, der ichs nicht sage"
(2) "Du machst mich allein," 63

9 *Six Bagatelles for String Quartet* (1913), ix, xxii, xxiv, 83, 127, 151

10 *Five Pieces for Orchestra* (1911-13), 81, 82-83, 128
Flute (piccolo), oboe, E-flat clarinet, clarinet (bass clarinet), horn, trumpet, trombone, percussion, xylophone, glockenspiel, bells, celesta, harp, harmonium, mandolin, guitar, violin, viola, cello, bass

11 *Three Small Pieces for Cello and Piano* (1914), viii, ix, 128

12 *Four Songs*, for high voice and piano (1915-17), viii, ix, xxii, 63, 128
(1) "Der Tag ist vergangen" (1915) (Folksong), 151
(2) "An einem Abend, da die Blumen dufteten" (1917), "Die geheimnisvolle Flöte" (Li-Tai-Po), from Hans Bethge, *Die chinesische Flöte*, xxii
(3) "Schien mir's, als ich sah die Sonne" (1915), from August Strindberg's *Ghost Sonata*
(4) "Ein Blumenglöckchen vom Boden hervor" (1917), from Goethe, *Gleich und Gleich*, xxii, 63

13 *Four Songs for Soprano and Orchestra* (1914-18), 63, 128-29, 149
Flute (piccolo), clarinet, bass clarinet, horn, trumpet, trombone, celesta, glockenspiel, harp, violin, viola, cello, bass

(1) "Wiese im Park" (Karl Kraus): "Wie wird mir zeitlos" (1917)
(2) "Die Einsame" (from Hans Bethge, *Die chinesische Flöte*): "An dunkelblauem Himmel steht der Mond" (1914)
(3) "In der Fremde" (*ibid.*): "In fremdem Land lag ich" (1917), 63
(4) "Ein Winterabend" (Georg Trakl): "Wenn der Schnee ans Fenster fällt" (1918), 63

13a The same, version for voice and piano, 15, 129

14 *Six Songs* (Georg Trakl), for high voice and instruments (1917-21), viii, xxvi, 129
E-flat (B-flat) clarinet, bass clarinet, violin, cello
(1) "Die Sonne": "Täglich kommt die gelbe Sonne" (1921)
(2) "Abendland I": "Mond, als träte ein Totes aus blauer Höhle" (1919)
(3) "Abendland II": "So leise sind die grünen Wälder unsrer Heimat" (1919)
(4) "Abendland III": "Ihr grossen Städte steinern aufgebaut" (1917)
(5) "Nachts": "Die Bläue meiner Augen ist erloschen" (1919)
(6) "Gesang einer gefangenen Amsel": "Dunkler Odem im grünen Gezweig" (1919)

14a The same, version for voice and piano, 15, 118, 129

15 *Five Sacred Songs,* for soprano and instruments (1917-22), viii, 8, 63, 91, 129-30
Flute, clarinet (bass clarinet), trumpet, harp, violin (viola)
(1) "Das Kreuz, das musst' er tragen"
(2) "Steht auf, ihr lieben Kindelein" ("Morgenlied," from *Des Knaben Wunderhorn*)
(3) "In Gottes Namen aufstehn," 8
(4) "Mein Weg geht jetzt vorüber"
(5) "Fahr hin, o Seel', zu deinem Gott" (double canon *in motu contrario*), 91

16 *Five Canons on Latin Texts,* for high soprano, clarinet, and bass clarinet (1923-24), viii, xxvi, 8, 92, 130
(1) "Christus factus est pro nobis," 8
(2) "Dormi Jesu, mater ridet" (from *Des Knaben Wunderhorn*)
(3) "Crux fidelis, inter omnes"
(4) "Asperges me, Domine"
(5) "Crucem tuam adoramus, Domine"

17 *Three Sacred Folksongs* (Three Traditional Rhymes) for voice, violin (viola), clarinet, and bass clarinet (1924), viii, xxvi, 55, 90, 130
(1) "Armer Sünder, du, die Erde ist dein Schuh"
(2) "Liebste Jungfrau, wir sind dein"
(3) "Heiland, unsre Missetaten," 55

18 *Three Songs,* for voice, E-flat clarinet, and guitar (1925), xxvi, 63, 130
(1) "Schatzerl klein, musst nit traurig sein"
(2) "Mein Kind, sieh an die Brüste mein ("Erlösung," from *Des Knaben Wunderhorn*), 63
(3) "Ave, Regina coelorum"

19 *Two Choral Songs* (Goethe), with instruments (1926), xxii, xxv, 62, 64-65, 71, 131, 151
Mixed chorus (SATB), clarinet, bass clarinet, celesta, guitar, violin
(1) "Weiss wie Lilien, reine Kerzen," 64
(2) "Zieh'n die Schafe von der Wiese," 64
From Goethe's *Chinesisch-Deutsche Jahres- und Tageszeiten*

20 *String Trio* (1927), xxvi, 93, 152
Violin, viola, cello
(1) Sehr langsam
(2) Sehr getragen und ausdrucksvoll

21 *Symphony* (1928), xxv, xxvi, xxvii, 10, 81, 83-85, 93-96
Clarinet, bass clarinet, 2 horns, harp, first and second violins, viola, cello
(1) Ruhig schreitend, 83-84, 93-95
(2) Variationen, 95-96

22 *Quartet,* with saxophone (1930), xxiii, 88, 96-100
Clarinet, tenor saxophone, violin, piano
(1) Sehr mässig, 96-99
(2) Sehr schwungvoll, 99-100

23 *Three Songs* from *Viae inviae* by Hildegard Jone, for medium voice and piano (1934), viii, 75, 151-52
(1) "Das dunkle Herz, das in sich lauscht"
(2) "Es stürzt aus Höhen Frische, die uns Leben macht"
(3) "Herr Jesus mein, Du trittst mit jedem Morgen ins Haus

24 *Concerto for Nine Instruments* (1934), xxiii, 10, 149
Flute, oboe, clarinet, horn, trumpet, trombone, violin, viola, piano

(1) Etwas lebhaft
(2) Sehr langsam
(3) Sehr rasch

25 *Three Songs* (Hildegard Jone), for high voice and piano (1934-35), viii, xxii
(1) "Wie bin ich froh!," xxii
(2) "Des Herzens Purpurvogel fliegt durch Nacht"
(3) "Sterne, ihr silbernen Bienen"

26 *Das Augenlicht* (Hildegard Jone), for mixed chorus and orchestra (1935), 62, 65-67, 69, 74, 100, 149, 152
Flute, oboe, clarinet, alto saxophone, horn, trumpet, trombone, timpani, xylophone, glockenspiel, cymbals, mandolin, celesta, harp, 8 violins, 4 violas, 4 cellos
"Durch unsre offnen Augen fliesst das Licht ins Herz"

27 *Variations for Piano* (1936), viii, xxiii, 10, 11, 14, 100
(1) Sehr mässig
(2) Sehr schnell
(3) Ruhig fliessend

28 *String Quartet* (1938), xxiii, 145-46
(1) Mässig
(2) Gemächlich
(3) Sehr fliessend

29 *First Cantata* (Hildegard Jone), for soprano solo, mixed chorus, and orchestra (1938-39), viii, ix, xxiii, 55, 62, 67-70, 71, 72, 74, 76, 81, 132-33
(1) SATB: "Zündender Lichtblitz des Lebens schlug," 67-69
(2) Soprano: "Kleiner Flügel, Ahornsamen, schwebst im Winde!"
(3) SATB: "Tönen die seligen Saiten Apolls," 69

30 *Variations for Orchestra* (1940), xxv, xxvi, 11-12, 13, 55, 80
Flute, oboe, clarinet, bass clarinet, horn, trumpet, trombone, tuba, timpani, celesta, harp, strings

31 *Second Cantata* (Hildegard Jone), for soprano and bass soli, mixed chorus, and orchestra (1941-43), xxiii, 15-16, 55, 62, 69, 70-76, 133, 155
Piccolo, flute, oboe, English horn, clarinet, bass clarinet, alto saxophone, bassoon, horn, trumpet, trombone, tuba, bells, glockenspiel, celesta, harp, strings
(1) Bass: "Schweigt auch die Welt," 70
(2) Bass: "Sehr tief verhalten," 15-16, 70

(3) SSA and Soprano: "Schöpfen aus Brunnen des Himmels," 15, 70, 71-72, 76
(4) Soprano: "Leichteste Bürde der Bäume," 71
(5) SATB and Soprano: "Freundselig ist das Wort," 71, 72-74, 76
(6) SATB: "Gelockert aus dem Schosse," 70, 71, 74-75

WORKS WITHOUT OPUS NUMBERS

The nine items thus far published are indicated as follows:
CF: Carl Fischer, Inc., 62 Cooper Square, New York 10003
UE: Universal Edition A.G., Karlsplatz 6, Vienna I, Austria
BB: Boelke-Bomart Music Publications, Inc., Hillsdale, New York

Opera
Alladine und Palomides, Maeterlinck (1908), sketch, 124-25

Orchestra
Im Sommerwind, idyll for large orchestra (1904) [CF], vii, x, xi, 17, 20-22, 43-52, 81, 123
Four Pieces (ca. 1910-13), 128
"Kräftig bewegt," F major, 136
"Sehr bewegt," D major, 136
Compositions for string orchestra, D minor, 137
Two movements in A minor, 137

Voice and Orchestra
Siegfrieds Schwert, ballade for solo voice and orchestra (1903), viii, 5, 17, 19, 43, 123
"O sanftes Glühn der Berge" (1913), 128
Two Songs (1914), 129
"O Mutter, Dank! So fühl ich deine Hand" (1919), sketch, 130

Wind and String Instruments
Composition (1925), 137

String Quartet
Langsamer Satz (1905) [CF], ix, 17, 22-23, 123
Quartet (1905) [CF] ix, 5, 17, 22, 23-27, 123
Quartet in A minor, sketches, 124
Rondo, 124
Minuet and Trio in A minor, 136
"Sehr bewegt," 137

String Trio
Satz für Streichtrio (1925) [UE], 130
String Trio (1925), sketch, 131
Quintet
Quintet for string quartet and piano (1906) [BB], 17, 27-28, 124
Violin and Piano
Extensive piece, 137
Violoncello and Piano
Two Pieces (1899), 122
Sonata (1914), 128
Piano Solo
Satz für Klavier (ca. 1905-6), sketches, 124
Kinderstück (1924), 130
Sonatensatz (ca. 1906), 124
Varia, 136
Songs, Voice and Piano
Three Poems (1899-1903) [CF], viii, 17, 122
(1) "Vorfrühling" (Ferdinand Avenarius)
(2) "Nachtgebet der Braut" (Richard Dehmel)
(3) "Fromm" (Gustav Falke)
Vorfrühling II (Avenarius), draft, 122
Two Songs after Poems by Ferdinand Avenarius (1900-1), 122
(1) "Wolkennacht"
(2) "Wehmut"
Three Songs after Poems by Ferdinand Avenarius (1903-4) [CF], viii, 17, 122
(1) "Gefunden"
(2) "Gebet"
(3) "Freunde"
Eight Early Songs (1901-4) [CF], viii, 17, 18, 122-23
(1) "Tief von Fern" (Richard Dehmel)
(2) "Aufblick" (Richard Dehmel), 18
(3) "Blumengruss" (Goethe), 18
(4) "Bild der Liebe" (Martin Greif)
(5) "Sommerabend" (Wilhelm Weigand)
(6) "Heiter" (Friedrich Nietzsche)
(7) "Der Tod" (Matthias Claudius)
(8) "Heimgang in der Frühe" (Detlev von Liliencron)
"Liebeslied" (Hans Böhm) (1904), fragment, 17n, 123

Five Songs after Poems by Richard Dehmel (1906-8) [CF], viii, xi, 17, 28-30, 53, 54, 55, 56-61, 124
(1) "Ideale Landschaft," 28, 56
(2) "Am Ufer," 56, 58
(3) "Himmelfahrt," 56, 59
(4) "Nächtliche Scheu," 56, 58
(5) "Helle Nacht," 29-30, 56, 59-61
Four Songs after Poems by Stefan George (1908-9), 126
(1) "Erwachen aus dem tiefsten Traumesschosse"
(2) "Kunfttag I"
(3) "Trauer I"
(4) "Das lockere Saatgefilde lechzet krank"
Early songs (uncatalogued), 136
Hochsommernacht, duo (Martin Greif), 122
Chorales
German chorales, 137

ARRANGEMENTS

The three items thus far published are indicated as follows:
UE: Universal Edition A.G., Karlsplatz 6, Vienna I, Austria

J. S. Bach
Ricercar a 6 voci (1935) [UE], xxv, 81-82, 144-45
No. 2 in the *Musical Offering;* orchestrated for flute, oboe, English horn, clarinet, bass clarinet, bassoon, horn, trumpet, trombone, timpani, harp, strings
Franz Schubert
Deutsche Tänze [UE], 145, 149
Arranged by Webern for 2 flutes, 2 oboes, 2 clarinets, 2 bassoons, 2 horns, and strings
"Romanze" from *Rosamunde*, voice and orchestra, 133
"Ihr Bild," voice and orchestra, 133
"Der Wegweiser," voice and orchestra, 133
"Du bist die Ruh," voice and orchestra, 134
"Thränenregen," voice and orchestra, 134
Three sonata movements, orchestra, 134
Franz Schubert and Hugo Wolf
Three Songs: see Wolf, "Lebe wohl"; Schubert, "Du bist die Ruh" and "Thränenregen"

SKETCHES